# A Life of
# FAVOR

# A Life of
# FAVOR

## A FAMILY THERAPIST EXAMINES THE
## STORY OF JOSEPH AND HIS BROTHERS

## RABBI RUSSELL RESNIK
### MA, LPCC

Lederer Books
A division of
Messianic Jewish Publishers
Clarksville, MD 21029

Printed in the United States of America
Cover design by Lisa Rubin,
Messianic Jewish Publishers
Graphic Design by Yvonne Vermillion,
Magic Graphix, Westfork, Arkansas


2017    1

ISBN: 978-1-936-71691-3

Library of Congress Control Number: 2017945194

Published by:

Lederer Books

A Division of Messianic Jewish Publishers & Resources

6120 Day Long Lane

Clarksville, MD 21029


Distributed by:

Messianic Jewish Publishers & Resources

Order line: (800) 410-7367

lederer@messianicjewish.net
www.MessianicJewish.net

*For my sons and daughters,*
*Luke, Daniel, Sarah, and Anna,*
*and their spouses and children.*
*May you all live lives of favor.*

# Table of Contents

# Preface

As I was wrapping up this writing project, I'd sometimes mention to friends or acquaintances that I was working on a book on the story of Joseph and his brothers. The most common response was something like, "Oh, I love that story!" or "That's one of my favorite stories in the Bible." This tale is undoubtedly one of the most beautiful and beloved stories in the Bible, and it's a gem of world literature. It spans a quarter of the whole book of Genesis, and is essential to understanding Genesis and all the Scriptures that follow. It's an indisputably great story, and most readers—Jewish, Christian, and unaffiliated—will already be familiar with it.

So, why do we need a new book that retells, or better, re-hears this familiar tale? The story of Jacob's sons points to a life of favor that can make a difference in our lives today. I don't believe we need to live with the depression, anxiety, and numerous addictions sweeping through our culture. But this is not a how-to book with easy steps to overcome these problems. Instead, it's a visionary book that looks deeply into this amazing story and helps us reimagine our own stories.

This deep reading and hearing of the story of Joseph and his brothers is unique in two major ways.

First, I pay special attention to the relational dynamics within Jacob's family. I'm a Messianic Jewish rabbi and also a clinical mental health counselor, with long experience in family dynamics and their implications for our daily lives. One reason for the endurance and popularity of Joseph's story is that it deals with struggles found in every family, including the recurring theme of sibling rivalry for the father's favor. This theme underlies what theologians call the doctrine of election—God's special choosing of a people, group or individual. But election is first a family issue before it is a theological one. Every child is born into a family and seeks favor—the approval and affirmation of family members, particularly the parents. Not everyone wants to be a Chosen One, as Joseph seems to become, but in Genesis, the conflicts over chosenness shed light on the universal struggle for favor, and the underlying drama of identity formation.. They also hint at a boundless favor, which is not to be won through sibling rivalry, but received as a gift. Reading the ancient story of Joseph and his brothers from a family-dynamics perspective provides rich insights into personal identity formation in the twenty-first century.

Second, I follow the story of Joseph and his brothers as it has been told and discussed among the Jewish people for many centuries, and engage with it at the same time as a follower of Yeshua the Messiah.

In the Jewish world, long before the Torah was divided into chapters and verses in the sixteenth century, it was divided into portions, or *parashiyot* (singular *parasha*). These portions are read each week in the synagogue, which ensures not only that the entire Torah is read aloud in the course of each year, but also that every synagogue in the world is reading the same portion at the same time. Over the years I've had friends, both Jewish and Gentile, who follow the reading cycle regularly. If we happen to run into each other at the gym or a coffee shop, we can immediately jump into a discussion of the weekly *parasha*. It's a great advantage of the annual reading cycle. Equally great is the millennia-long conversation among the Jewish sages that proceeds *parasha* by *parasha*, and invites us to join in if we're following the cycle of readings.

This millennial conversation has been shaped by *midrash*,[1] traditional Jewish interpretations of the biblical text, some of which go back to the very first centuries of the Common Era. The word midrash is derived from the Hebrew root *DARASH*, which means to seek, inquire, or explain.[2] Midrash is the result of such textual exploration, always balanced by the rabbinic dictum, "A verse cannot depart from its plain meaning" (b.Shabbat 63a). The imaginative readings of Midrash don't set aside the plain meaning of a text, but rather develop possible implications and applications that *go beyond* it. Since we will draw heavily upon Midrash as we follow Joseph's story, I should explain the benefits of this approach.

▶ Inviting the ancient sages of Midrash into our reading of Genesis is giving a voice to those who have gone before us, as the great 20th-century Christian author G.K. Chesterton wrote: "Tradition means giving a vote to the most obscure of all classes, our ancestors. It is the democracy of the dead."[3] If this was an apt saying in 1908, when it was first published, it's even more relevant today, when we're far more captivated by whatever is the latest and most up-to-date. Midrash represents the voice of my Jewish ancestors, and I want to honor them by listening carefully to them.

▶ I'm bringing a current perspective—family dynamics—into our reading of the story, and I want to make sure I'm not just reading this modern idea back into the ancient tales of Torah. By listening to the interpretations and insights of pre-modern students of the text, I can avoid distorting it with my distinctly 21st-century concerns.

► Midrash, and Jewish scholars in general, pay close attention to narrative and the literary riches it involves. Christian commentators tend to be more eager to trace abstract principles and resolve inconsistencies in the text than to let the story carry us along. But storytelling, with all of its subtleties and nuances, is a particularly powerful way to convey truth in our postmodern culture, and Midrash, whether or not we agree with all its particulars, provides a master key to hearing the story.

As I noted above, even as I draw deeply upon Midrash and other Jewish sources, I remain thoroughly Messianic in my perspective. That is, I believe Yeshua of Nazareth is the Messiah promised throughout the Tanakh.[4] Fusing a Yeshua-positive perspective with a deep Jewish reading of the story is part of what makes this book unique.

The tale of Joseph and his brothers is a true story first recorded by the hand of Moses, as part of the Torah (Genesis through Deuteronomy) he received at Mount Sinai. In this book, we'll gain insights into the story from a family-dynamics perspective and explore it more deeply through the Midrash, but through it all we'll be listening to a story. For this reason I will sometimes refer to the Narrator who tells this tale. The story is timeless, and picturing a living Narrator or storyteller rather than the historical figure of Moses helps us realize how alive and current this ancient tale really is.

Midrash follows the divisions of the *parashiyot*, which often make more sense than the chapter divisions developed much later. Each *parasha* is named after one of the first words in its text, and this name usually makes good sense interpretively. Accordingly, the first four chapters of this book after the introduction will reflect the four *parashiyot* that comprise the story of Joseph and his brothers. The final chapter explores the implications of this story for our personal lives, families, and communities today.

### *Vayeshev* "And he settled." Genesis 37:1–40:23

Jacob returns from a long exile (Genesis 28–35) and settles in the Land of Canaan, the land promised to him and his ancestors, but his family troubles continue there. During his exile, he fathered eleven sons and one daughter. His twelfth son, Benjamin, is born in the Land of Canaan to Rachel, Jacob's favored wife, who dies in childbirth. Just as he favored Rachel, Jacob openly favors Rachel's older son, Joseph, which stirs up deep resentment among the other ten brothers. Joseph has two dreams of having dominion over his brothers and even his parents, and unwisely tells his whole family about them. When the opportunity arises, the brothers get rid of Joseph by selling him to traders, who bring him down to Egypt as a slave. The story's focus shifts briefly to Judah, a contender for the lead role among the brothers, to tell of the birth of his two sons, Peretz and Zerach. The narrative returns to Egypt, where Joseph ends up in prison. There he accurately interprets the dreams of two fellow prisoners, who were servants of Pharaoh. He asks the prisoner who is about to be released to remember him when he is restored to Pharaoh's service, but he forgets about Joseph.

### *Mikketz* "At the end." Genesis 41:1–44:17

At the end of two more years of Joseph's imprisonment, Pharaoh has a troubling pair of dreams that no one can interpret. The ex-prisoner remembers Joseph and tells Pharaoh, who has him summoned from prison. Joseph stands before Pharaoh, interprets his dreams with undeniable accuracy, and recommends a plan of action to deal with the famine the dreams predict. Pharaoh appoints Joseph to be in charge of this plan, and gives him full authority as his right-hand man. As the famine progresses, Joseph's brothers come to Egypt to buy food, but they don't recognize him. He initiates a complex test to see whether the brothers have changed since betraying him 22 years earlier. The test ends with Joseph taking Benjamin captive and offering freedom to the rest of the brothers.

### *Vayigash* "And he drew near." Genesis 44:18–47:27

Judah draws near to Joseph with a bold offer to become Joseph's slave in place of Benjamin. Through Judah, the brothers pass Joseph's test, and he finally reveals himself to them. Joseph arranges for Jacob to rejoin him in Egypt, and the family is reunited there. Joseph introduces his brothers, and then his father, to Pharaoh, and they receive the right to dwell in Egypt, where they thrive and multiply. Joseph completes his famine-relief plan, which greatly increases the power of Pharaoh.

### *Vayechi* "And he lived." Genesis 47:28–50:26

Jacob lives in Egypt for 17 years after being reunited with Joseph. He has time to speak a prophetic blessing over each of his sons and arrange to be buried in the Promised Land. After Jacob's death, Joseph reassures his brothers that he had long ago forgiven them for their betrayal, and comforts them. Before he dies, Joseph foretells their eventual departure from Egypt, and directs them to take his bones with them for burial with his ancestors. The story concludes: "So Yosef died at the age of 110, and they embalmed him and put him in a coffin in Egypt."

## Conclusion: A life of favor

Our forefathers, Abraham, Isaac, and Jacob, all practiced favor, sometimes wisely and often unwisely, but always as an inseparable part of who they were as fathers. In this they reflected the fatherhood of God, who had favored them and chosen them to have a universal redemptive impact. In the Bible, God reveals himself to the world, and acts within the world, through a favored family, which becomes a favored nation that brings forth a favored son who will have a redemptive impact on all the families of humankind. Identity founded on trust in the Father and his boundless favor transforms the way we relate to ourselves, our families, and our whole community. How do I enter this life of favor? How do I discover and maintain a favor-based identity? We'll conclude our exploration of the story of Joseph and his brothers with a paradox: I get hold of boundless favor by giving boundless favor to others.

# Introduction

My friend Bernie was a Jew from Brooklyn who became a follower of Yeshua in mid-life, and died at 93. After his burial, friends held a service that included time to share their memories of Bernie. The man moderating the service said, "Bernie always called me 'my man,'" and then he joked, "I'm sure he didn't ever say that to anyone else. In fact, he said to me, 'You're my main man.'" But then another man stood up and said, "Bernie called *me* 'my man.' I thought I was the only one!" That friendly competition became a lighthearted theme of the service, relieving some of the sadness of losing Bernie. But I've attended other funerals where the competition among mourners for recognition of their unique place in the life of the departed was not so friendly. At these funerals, memories were shared not only to honor the loved one, but also to imply how this or that mourner was entitled to a special portion of that honor.

This behavior reflects a deep human longing that goes back to ancient times—the desire to be favored, to be chosen, by a leader or parent. It's a desire rooted in our biology, the need to not only be part of a family or tribe, but to really *belong*. I say this theme goes back to ancient times because it is already well-established in the Bible, including in the very first book, Genesis, or *B'reisheet*—"in the beginning." The theme of favor resounds throughout Genesis, along with the theme of competition for that favor, which we today call "sibling rivalry". Underlying this drama of disputed favor, the story hints at what I call "boundless favor"—favor that doesn't need to be gained through competition and cunning, but is given freely—an unlimited resource. In the family stories of Genesis, this boundless favor is a subtext, sometimes only a hint, but it's there, and it will become a bright and hopeful theme if we pay close attention to the saga and to the family dynamics at play within it.

Early in Genesis, God chooses one man, Abraham,[1] out of the whole human race to be uniquely blessed and to become a source of blessing to all. It's not just a choice of one man, however, but of a family. One of Abraham's sons, Isaac, is chosen to receive and transmit the blessing, even though he is not the firstborn. Likewise, Isaac's second-born son Jacob is chosen over the firstborn Esau. This book focuses on the story of Jacob's sons, Joseph and his brothers, which portrays family dynamics and the rivalry for favor in profound detail. Before we get into that story, however, let's get a picture of its wider context, the entire book of Genesis.

## The mother road of God's purpose

I live in New Mexico, Albuquerque to be exact, about a mile north of old Route 66, America's "Mother Road" from the '30s through the '60s, linking Chicago and Los Angeles across the vast stretches of prairie and high desert in between. It's easy for me to imagine God's purpose in the book of Genesis as a Mother Road setting out from "In the beginning" toward its ultimate destination; a highway glinting in the sunlight as it disappears over the western horizon on the way to the Age to Come. This highway bears God's purpose from the very beginning: to create humankind as bearers of the divine image, and bless them with fruitfulness and dominion, so that the image of God is reflected throughout his entire creation. But this purpose meets with various obstacles, beginning with the catastrophic disobedience of the first man and woman. They are expelled from the Garden and sent into exile. There, their firstborn son kills his younger brother, out of resentment that God had favored him. This initial act of sibling rivalry will be repeated, and it will deeply threaten God's purpose of blessing. The purpose remains, however, throughout Genesis and its multiple challenges—the depravity of Noah's generation, the rebellion of the builders of the Tower of Babel, the conflicts within the chosen line of Abraham—the highway of God's from-the-beginning purpose of blessing stretches into the future.

One Hebrew word, *Toldot*, provides a marker all along this highway. Usually translated as "generations," this key word appears ten times in Genesis, in the phrase *eleh toldot*, or "these are the generations." The story of Joseph and his brothers opens in Genesis 37:2 with the last of these ten occurrences. Like many Hebrew words in the Bible, *toldot* can't be translated with the same English word every time it's used. Sometimes it introduces a series of events, or a story, as in its first appearance, in Genesis 2:4: "*Eleh toldot*, this is what came forth from the heavens and the earth when they were created" (my translation). Here I translate *toldot* as "what came forth," but the JPS TANAKH renders it, "Such is *the story* of heaven and earth..." (emphasis added). Commentator Nahum Sarna writes: "In each of its other ten occurrences, it introduces what follows, invariably in close connection with the name of a person already mentioned in the narrative. Its use indicates that a new and significant development is at hand."[2] The ten other occurrences of *toldot* include its final appearance: "This is the story of Jacob: Joseph, being seventeen years old, tended the flock with his brothers..." (37:2, my translation).

The phrase *eleh toldot* serves as a sort of chapter divider in the narratives of Genesis. Some of these chapters are long, like the account of the family of Terah, father of Abraham (11:27), or the family of Jacob, father of Joseph (37:2). Others are short, like the paragraphs devoted to the families of Ishmael (25:12) and Esau (36:1). But rather than forming ordinary chapters, the sections introduced by *eleh toldot* mark off the great highway of Genesis, with all its sections linked together as records of the extended clan of Abraham. This structure reveals Genesis, the first and foundational book of the Bible, is above all a story of family, and this is one reason it has remained so relevant and compelling throughout the ages.

Like Route 66, the great highway of Genesis intersects with various side roads, but the mother road is the family narrative of Abraham, which begins with his father, Terah, in 11:27. The side roads that are also marked by the *eleh toldot* sign, such as the lines of Ishmael and Esau, aren't dead ends. They also receive a share of God's blessing in the here-and-now, and are headed toward a share in the greater blessing to come through the chosen family of Abraham. Other side roads, like the lines of Cain or Ham, remain unmarked, or eventually drop out of sight altogether. The mother road marked out by the line of Abraham, Isaac, and Jacob is the one chosen by God to accomplish his purpose for the entire human race, and it's a purpose revealed through the family dynamics of this chosen line.

## The firstborn and the favored

Genesis 5 provides a key to understanding the mother road of Genesis and how it applies to our lives today.

> This is the record of Adam's line.—When God created man, He made him in the likeness of God; male and female He created them. And when they were created, He blessed them and called them Man.—When Adam had lived 130 years, he begot a son in his likeness after his image, and he named him Seth. (Gen. 5:1–3, JPS TANAKH)

The passage ends with Adam begetting Seth, but of course, Seth isn't Adam's first son; he's the third. Cain is the firstborn, but *Seth* is the one Genesis says is begotten in Adam's likeness after his image—that is, the one through whom the original blessing-purpose of God will go forward. God had passed over Cain and his offering and favored Abel and his offering. After Cain murdered Abel in a jealous rage, the inheritance passed to the third son, setting a pattern that prevails throughout Genesis and beyond. In the line of Abraham, the purpose is transmitted through the later-born and unlikely son, rather than the one who might be expected to be the heir. This is a feature of the ten *eleh toldot* verses in Genesis, which we moderns might miss because we don't pay the kind of attention to birth order that our biblical ancestors did. The *minor* roads represent the lines of the firstborn; the major highway follows the route marked by the later-born, the offspring of the barren one, the unlikely heir. And because these are unlikely heirs, their rise stirs up an often-fierce sibling rivalry.

As moderns, we might forget that the firstborn is the one intended and expected to carry forward the legacy to the coming generations, the one who is automatically favored. But this was a cardinal principle in the ancient Near East, and among the

Hebrews in particular. It became enshrined in the ordinances of Torah itself, as for example in Deuteronomy 21:15–17:

> If a man has two wives, the one loved and the other unloved, and both the loved and unloved wives have borne him children, and if the firstborn son is the child of the unloved wife; then, when it comes time for him to pass his inheritance on to his sons, he may not give the inheritance due the firstborn to the son of the loved wife in place of the son of the unloved one, who is in fact the firstborn. No, he must acknowledge as firstborn the son of the unloved wife by giving him a double portion of everything he owns, for he is the firstfruits of his manhood, and the right of the firstborn is his.[3]

In a sin-disordered world, however, this normal expectation isn't always fulfilled. God sometimes chooses another son, to make it clear that his purposes will prevail even if they must reverse the normal course of human society.

> In Israel, as in much of the rest of the ancient near east, the firstborn son, Reuben, enjoyed a position of honor and favor. He is called "the first of the (procreative) strength" of the father (Gen 49:3). So noteworthy were departures from this rule, that they became, in C. H. Gordon's words, "worthy of saga." As such these departures constitute a literary theme in the Bible (Gen 25:23; etc.). . . . The Lord's choice of Abel over Cain, of Jacob over Esau, of Joseph and Judah over Reuben, of Ephraim over Manasseh, of Moses over Aaron, of David over his brothers, of Solomon over Adonijah, show that he is the Lord of sacred history and that he transcends cultural norms.[4]

The "departures" from the rule of the firstborn not only constitute a literary theme in the Bible, but they also help give the Bible its profound and compelling literary quality, its drama. Furthermore, the saga of the favored son versus the firstborn son reflects the drama of sibling rivalry, starting with Cain and Abel, and continuing in our families to this day. In my counseling practice, I've observed that the dynamics that begin with rivalry in the family of origin, especially comparison and competition between the kids, play out in later life and relationships, including the new family, the business world, and congregations as well. Sometimes a child wonders not only, "Does Daddy love me?" but, "Does Daddy love me as much as he loves my big brother?" This child grows up believing he needs to compete for his father's love . . . or he gives up on ever winning it and goes off into rebellion or estrangement from the family.

Rabbi Jonathan Sacks argues that this sibling rivalry is inherent to the human condition, and is perhaps even more basic than the father-son conflict emphasized by Freud and his followers.

> The primal act of violence is fratricide not parricide [murder of the father]. Sibling rivalry plays a central role in human conflict, and it begins with mimetic desire, the desire to have what your brother has, or even be what your brother is.[5]

Underlying this "primal act of violence" is an equally primal drive for identity, the need to know who you are, and have others know who you are, in the midst of a complex, often chaotic world. As Rabbi Sacks notes, sibling rivalry isn't just a desire to have what our brother has, but to *be* what our brother *is*—to have a viable identity even if we get it at our brother's expense. The drama of firstborn versus favored captures this abiding struggle and runs throughout Genesis to reach its climax with the final *eleh toldot*: "This is the line of Jacob: Joseph..." (Gen. 37:2).

## The quest for favor

I've been using "chosen" and "favored" almost interchangeably, and will continue to do so throughout this book, but they're not quite synonymous. Neither term is defined abstractly in Genesis, but both are essential to the story and defined by their usage within it.[6] Let's consider "favor" first.

Favor is undeserved kindness. It can come from God or man. One Hebrew term often translated as "favor" is *chen* (with the guttural *ch* as in Bach), and this word can help us gain an understanding of the whole concept. For example, *chen* appears four times in the brief description of the encounter between Jacob and Esau (Gen. 33:5–11). Jacob returns from his twenty-year sojourn in Paddan-Aram with abundant flocks and a huge family. Esau asks who all these people are, and Jacob answers, "The children with whom God has *favored* your servant." Jacob uses the same word two more times to ask for favor from Esau, and then a final time to reiterate God's favor. Jacob is saying that God in his kindness has given him more than he deserves. Then Jacob asks Esau to also give him something he doesn't deserve, by accepting his gift and thereby making peace with him. Favor in this sense is a direct contradiction to the idea that I have to compete with my siblings—or anyone else—for any good I might receive in life. Instead, the good things come as a gift.

The Hebrew term *chen* appears only once in Joseph's story, but it sheds light on the whole narrative. As we'll hear later, Joseph spends time in prison after being wrongly accused. There, "the LORD was with Joseph and extended mercy to him, and gave him *favor* in the eyes of the ruler of the prison" (Gen. 39:21, literal translation). Favor here isn't something Joseph had to earn or compete for. He gets it because the LORD is with him and gives him mercy, a break he doesn't deserve. Because of this favor, Joseph is quickly elevated to a position of authority second only to the prison-keeper's. "As in ch 37, which speaks of Jacob's preference for Joseph (vv. 3–4), so here the latter is the beneficiary of a mysterious *favor*, this time from the LORD."[7] Because of this mysterious favor, Joseph is successful in all he does, and rises quickly wherever he finds himself. This favor will lead to his elevation to second-in-command under Pharaoh, but it began back when Joseph was just a youth, and received favor from his father. The sense of favor, which we might seek from the LORD, has its roots in the favor we experience—or long for—within our own families.

Favor is undeserved kindness. We use the term in the same sense today when we ask someone to do us a favor. This usage hints at the idea of boundless favor that doesn't have to be earned or doled out by measure, but reflects the generosity of God himself. Of course, I'm not thinking in such lofty terms when I ask my friend to bring me a cup of coffee while he's up getting one for himself, or to check in his car for a notebook I think I left there. My friend might do this grudgingly, and even keep score, but God's favor, by definition, is given freely and with no strings attached. We humans might have to stretch to do someone a favor, but God's favor is part of his very nature.

Being chosen is a result of this favor. God's favor is upon Joseph, and because of it, he is repeatedly chosen for a special assignment. Of course, we could put this the other way around—because God has chosen Joseph, he receives special favor. To further complicate things, God's favor and human favor often get confused. Joseph isn't just favored by God, he's also favored by his father, Jacob. His brothers resent Jacob's favor, but apparently don't consider whether it might reflect God's favor, whether it's something they should honor rather than resent. If we're honest with ourselves, it's not hard to understand the brothers' resentment. It does some unfair that Joseph gets all that favor and that Jacob is so obvious with his favoritism. And if we're even more honest, we might admit that God's favor seems unfair sometimes. As we examine the story of Joseph and his brothers, we'll explore such responses to the apparent unfairness of favor and discover new ways to respond.

In the story of Abraham and his family, with all its twists and turns, favor and chosenness are not only interrelated, but together constitute a major theme. This ancient theme remains active today, as it was at Bernie's funeral, which poked fun at the sort of competition for favor that rages within many families to this day. And we can look beyond family life to the relationship between religious groups and nationalities, where the competition for favor, the competition to be the chosen one, has often turned deadly. We can think of recent terror attacks by Islamist groups throughout the world—where the attackers often target Christians or Jews—or the atrocities of the Islamic State in the Middle East—where Christians and other religious minorities are butchered just because of who they are. These atrocities are committed to fulfill the terrorists' sense of being chosen for a "God-given mission." These are hideously extreme examples, which even the worst family conflicts we may encounter only dimly reflect. Nevertheless, they illustrate the widespread view that being chosen is a zero-sum matter, in which favor toward one requires the rejection of the other. In this view, favor produces a winner and a loser, or many losers, and because of it, the rivalry for favor remains just as intense and divisive today as it was in Joseph's time. But the stories of Genesis that portray this rivalry, if we read them with care, also point to a way beyond zero-sum favor and the rivalry it produces, to the way of boundless favor that can change our lives today.

## The quest for identity

We would all probably like our families to be the scenes of boundless favor for all members. We'd all like to have a safe place where I belong, where I'll be loved and affirmed regardless of my behavior. But this family ideal isn't always the reality. Sooner or later the son or daughter makes the bitter discovery that even here in the family, favor will be parceled out, with strings attached. And beneath the resulting competition for love and approval is an even deeper struggle to form an identity, to be someone and belong somewhere. The stories of Genesis recognize this sense of identity is not a given in most families throughout history, but must be earned, often at the expense of others. The stories also hint at a better way to form identity.

As we saw above, Rabbi Sacks ties sibling rivalry to a drive he calls *mimetic desire*, "the desire to have what your brother has, or even be what your brother is."[8] Wanting to be what your brother is—namely, the favored one—perfectly captures the rivalry between Joseph and his brothers, just as it captures the sibling rivalry his father (Jacob vs. Esau) and grandfather (Isaac vs. Ishmael) experienced. And it remains a dynamic in the rivalries of our own times. This struggle for favor is not the product of ancient, primitive cultures, but is something inherent within the human heart—the deep yearning to be affirmed by another human being, which begins with the instinctual yearning for the affirmation of a mother and father.

Wanting to be what someone else is also points to the struggle for identity formation. Like sibling rivalry, this is a modern term, but it has a long history. I may be part of a family, tribe, or even a mighty kingdom, but where do I individually fit in? How do I stand out within the group to which I belong? "In all cultures, the family imprints its members with selfhood. Human experience of identity has two elements: a sense of belonging and a sense of being separate."[9] *Selfhood* and *identity* in this passage are similar terms. *Selfhood* should not be confused with selfishness or self-preoccupation. It means having enough awareness and personal definition to take responsibility in life, to function in the world, and to relate to other "selves." *Identity* provides that kind of definition through belonging to a family or family-like group, and distinguishing oneself or standing out, within that family or group.

## The hero's journey

The search for selfhood or identity, which remains so relevant today, has been expressed from the earliest times, in ancient myths and legends as the tale of the hero's journey.[10] The hero leaves home, passes into an alien and often mysterious realm, overcomes great trials, often including near-death experiences, and is finally raised up out of the trials to return home with great powers that benefit his family and people. On the way, the hero often finds a mentor or supernatural guide, and most of all, his or her true identity.

J.R.R. Tolkien's *The Lord of the Rings* is a complex, deeply layered hero's-journey tale. Tolkien's ability to bring this ancient theme of identity formation to life is a key to the story's unparalleled popularity and impact. The hobbit Frodo becomes the unlikely hero when he comes into possession of a mysterious ring. He learns from his mentor Gandalf that this is the One Ring, which threatens all of Middle-earth, and must be carried to "the Cracks of Doom" in far-off Mordor to be destroyed. Since Frodo has come into possession of the Ring, he is the one who must destroy it. "I am not made for perilous quests," Frodo protests. "I wish I had never seen the Ring! Why did it come to me? Why was I chosen?"[11] Nevertheless, he accepts his mission, and leaves his homeland, the Shire, to journey through alien and mysterious realms, where he endures great danger, captivity, and a nearly mortal wound. It's a transformative journey for Frodo, who is somehow empowered to find the Cracks of Doom and fulfill his mission. But even after the Ring is destroyed, even after his friend Aragorn is crowned as the rightful King, Frodo must return to the Shire to rescue it from the oppressive regime that took over after his departure. He saved all of Middle-earth, but he must return home to save the little corner of Middle-earth called the Shire.

This same kind of journey appears in the stories of our biblical ancestors—not because the Bible is copying ancient legends, but because both the legends and inspired Scripture are reflecting the universal quest to find oneself.

So, translator Everett Fox titles Genesis 12:1–9 "The Call and the Journey," commenting: "The Avraham cycle begins decisively, with a command from God to leave the past behind and go to an unnamed land." Fox notes, however, "The classic mythological motif of the journey, where the hero meets such dangers as monsters and giants, has here been avoided."[12] The biblical stories are not myths, but like the mythic journey stories, they reveal deep spiritual and psychological truths. As Fox notes, "Yaakov's journey takes him not only to a foreign land, but to the portals of adulthood."[13] Joseph will have a similar journey. He is exiled from his homeland into a completely different realm. There he suffers slavery and imprisonment until he is finally raised up and empowered to be a source of blessing and salvation to his family, as well as to all the surrounding nations. Notably, Joseph doesn't return home, but instead summons "home"— that is, his family—to himself in Egypt. Only after death, and after the close of Genesis, will he return home as his brothers carry his bones back to the Promised Land for burial.

The hero's journey story builds upon the two dynamics of identity formation we still experience today: the sense of belonging and the sense of being separate. The hero must separate from his family to find himself, and he also must return, so that he still belongs, even after the journey of separation. His separation empowers him to eventually return as a source of blessing and help. Through his journey, he becomes his own person, not just for his own sake, but to benefit the family, tribe, and community. The hero's journey also sets him or her apart from the siblings, resolving the issue of sibling rivalry, often in ways that benefit all the siblings.

In modern culture, the sense of being separate is heightened and has countless ways to express itself—and to drive parents crazy. On the other hand, in our times, with family structures so deteriorated, the sense of belonging is much weaker, so perhaps sibling rivalry is not as pronounced as in biblical times. As children get older, they tend to distance themselves from family much more than in the past. But the quest for identity and the need to answer "Who am I?" may be more intense than ever. All this keeps the original family stories of Genesis up-to-date and relevant, even despite the growing unbelief and secularism of the 21st century. These stories reflect a quest for identity still rooted in the hearts of individuals everywhere. In an age in which people are more confused about identity than ever before, when identity is seen as strictly a matter of personal choice, an accessory to be put on or taken off at will, we have much to learn from the ancient tales of identity formation.

One of the key lessons, in fact, is simply that true identity requires a journey. Despite the claims of postmodern culture, identity really isn't something you can just choose and put on, or take off, at will. Authentic identity is given by God. For many Jews, identity comes from being part of the Jewish people, and from accepting the responsibilities and blessings that come with that participation. Christians see their identity as based on union with Christ. (Messianic Jews, like myself, embrace both identities.) But even such God-given identity must be tested and proven, if the individual is to really own it. Parents are often frustrated by that reality, as they do all they can to raise their children with a sense of who they are in God, and their children just don't seem to get it, or only get it after years of wandering and self-inflicted difficulties. Every child has to discover who he or she is as an individual, and the journey—long, arduous and challenging—remains a powerful image for the process of identity formation.

## From Cain and Abel to Joseph and his brothers

As we saw, the first recorded conflict between two humans was sparked by a dispute over favor, when God favored Abel over Cain. This kind of conflict extends not only throughout the length of Genesis, but throughout the history of sons of Israel. God will favor Abraham, Isaac, and Jacob as decisively as he favors Abel. He will rename Jacob "Israel" and choose his offspring, the tribes of Israel, in perpetuity, a choice that sets the stage for the next book of the Bible, Exodus, and for the rest of Scripture. The Cain and Abel story also reveals the hostility, envy, and worse, that God's favor often stirs up in the one not favored—a theme throughout Scripture that remains alive to this day. Nonetheless, winning the competition for favor and becoming the chosen one is a burden as well as a blessing. Joseph's story reveals that the path of the chosen one—like the path of the chosen people throughout history—isn't smooth and direct. It is filled with setbacks, pitfalls (sometimes literal) and trials, sometimes created by the chosen one himself.

In addition, the story of Cain and Abel implies that favoring one doesn't always mean rejecting the other. I don't have to find or form my identity at the expense of someone else. God pays no heed to Cain and his offering, yet he reaches out to Cain, "Why are you angry? Why so downcast? If you are doing what is good, shouldn't you hold your head high?" (4:7). Even before Cain responds, or fails to, God is communicating with him and seeking his best. And regardless of Cain's response, God remains who he is, the God of order and truth who calls it like it is, but who is also compassionate and quick to forgive. He urges Cain to define who he is—to gain an identity—not based on rejection and anger, but on doing what is good.

God's favor of one does not entail the rejection of all the rest. This truth is part of the equation of boundless favor. It will come into focus in the story of Joseph and his brothers, but it's difficult for human beings to grasp, with our inborn tendency to compare and compete, to imagine life as a zero-sum game in which your advance requires my decline, and vice versa. Genesis at times seems to reflect this all-too-common view, but it also portrays a way of life far beyond this view, the way of boundless favor. God's favor toward one, and the sufferings of that favored one, will produce good for the many who aren't favored in that way. Joseph's brothers try to undo his favored position, but he tells them at the end of his story, "You meant to do me harm, but God meant it for good—so that it would come about as it is today, with many people's lives being saved" (50:20). The reality God's favor, which is still at work in the world today, can be life-giving, as it will turn out to be for the family of Jacob. But before we can reach this conclusion, we have a long and rocky road to travel with Joseph, a road that opens up when he is a seventeen-year-old youth.

# Chapter One

# *Vayeshev*
# "And he settled"

*And Ya'akov settled in the land where his father
had lived as a foreigner, the land of Kena'an.*

Our parasha opens with words that sound like the end of the
story, a "happily-ever-after" ending for Jacob. Years before, he
had been driven out from this same land, endured many trials and
adventures, and was finally able to return. Now, at last, he is
settled in the land. The very next verse, however, gets the story
moving again, and it doesn't look like it's headed toward a happy
ending. Jacob's 17-year-old son Joseph brings him a bad report
about some of his older brothers. Jacob loves Joseph more than
these brothers, his other sons, and gives him a special robe to
mark his favor. The brothers can see with their own eyes that
their father loves Joseph above all of them, and "they began to
hate him and reached the point where they couldn't even talk
with him in a civil manner" (37:4).

The story that follows is the final leg of the great Mother
Road of Genesis discussed in the Introduction. The road is
marked by the phrase *Eleh toldot*, "These are the generations."
Now in Hebrew we hear just four words, *Eleh toldot Ya'akov
Yoseph*, literally, "These are the generations of Jacob, Joseph."

The outcome of Jacob's whole struggle to create and nurture a family in the unfriendly surroundings of his uncle Laban is embodied in this one son of his. Joseph is apparently chosen to bear the legacy of his father, and therefore of his ancestors Isaac and Abraham as well, upon his skinny 17-year-old shoulders. Joseph's identity is clear: As a family therapist might put it, he *belongs* to the lineage of Abraham, Isaac and Jacob, and has a sense of *being separate* through the special favor he receives.[1] But he handles that favor in a way that will make the whole story go terribly awry—or so it will seem.

## The garment of favor

"Now Isra'el loved Yosef the most of all his children, because he was the son of his old age; and he made him a long-sleeved robe" (37:3). This long-sleeved robe is *ketonet passim* in Hebrew. This term has been translated in various ways: an ornamented tunic, a garment of fine wool, or in the beautiful rendering of the King James Version, "a coat of many colours." Whatever its exact description, it was a unique and valuable garment that Jacob gave his son, definitely not the ordinary clothing of the day, but a noble tunic.

A *ketonet passim* makes only one other appearance in the Tanakh, in the story of Tamar and her half-brother Amnon (2 Sam. 13). Amnon becomes infatuated with Tamar, tricks her into entering his bedroom, and rapes her. Then he rejects her and has her thrown out of his house. The story continues: "She was wearing a *ketonet passim*, for so were dressed daughters of the king who were virgins. Then his servant took her outside and barred the door after her. Tamar put dust on her head and tore the *ketonet passim* she was wearing; she put her hands on her head, and walked away, crying out as she went" (vv. 18–19, literal translation).

Whatever the exact nature of the *ketonet passim*, it was clearly worn to mark the status of the king's virgin daughters. Tearing or rending the garment was the customary sign of mourning in ancient Israel. Later in the story of Joseph, when Jacob is tricked into believing Joseph is dead, his first response is to tear his garments (37:33–35). This act has public significance; the mourner cannot present himself within the community as fully and normally clothed when he is bearing the profound loss of the death of a loved one, or as in Tamar's case, the loss of her virginity (and hence, in her world, eligibility for marriage). But the Narrator makes a point of telling us not only that Tamar rends her garment, but that this garment is the *ketonet passim*. Tamar's rending of the garment not only signifies her mourning, it also announces the loss of her public status as a virgin daughter of the king. The garment cannot remain whole when she is defiled.

## Jacob's favor

Perhaps we shouldn't fault Jacob for favoring Joseph, because this is a father's prerogative, but he *can* be faulted for displaying his favor so blatantly, and dressing up his favorite son with a visible status-marker at the expense of his other sons. Jacob seems blind to the sibling rivalry brewing among his sons—perhaps because he grew up with the very same rivalry himself. Could it be that Jacob shows such overt favoritism toward one of his sons because of his own experience growing up? The Narrator describes Jacob's favor simply enough: "Now Isra'el loved Yosef the most of all his children" (37:3). And he's just as direct in describing Jacob's relationship with his parents: Literally, "Yitz'chak *favored* 'Esav, because he had a taste for game; Rivkah *favored* Ya'akov" (25:28, emphasis added). As a child, Jacob learned that, in his family at least, parental favor was a limited commodity, a commodity for which he had to compete—and the competition got pretty rough. Jacob ended up with the signs of favor—the family birthright and his father's blessing—but might still have wondered how much his father loved him. After all, when Isaac sent Jacob off to Paddan-Aram to find a wife, he blessed him, but sent him alone, on foot, without the abundant gifts that had enabled Isaac to obtain his wife years before (Gen. 28:1–5). Jacob will have to work with his own hands for seven years to earn the bride-price.

Young Jacob's status as the favored one, then, was dubious. He obtained the perks of the favored status through manipulation, but he still had to wonder whether his father really loved him above his brother Esau. Notice I said "above" his brother instead of "as much as" or "along with" his brother. Jacob's experience of favor was that it's hard to get and can't be spread around. If I win it, you lose it, and vice versa. It remains even to this day a painful—but not unusual—way to grow up. In the modern West, signs of favor such as Jacob gained are usually not so obvious. But I've sometimes spoken with a young parent who feels that the children of an older sister get all the grandparents' attention, while their own are left out in the cold. Another person might have a younger brother who can do no wrong in his parents' eyes, even though everyone else recognizes him as a troubled and self-indulgent kid.

The dynamics of such favoritism played out in Jacob's dual marriage to Leah and Rachel. As soon as Jacob arrived in "the land of the people of the east," he met Rachel at a well and helped her water her father's sheep. And then, "Ya'akov kissed Rachel and wept aloud. Ya'akov told Rachel that he was her father's relative, and that he was Rivkah's son; and she ran and told her father" (29:11–12). Jacob loved Rachel and agreed to work for her father, Laban, for seven years in exchange for her bride-price (since Jacob's father sent him off empty-handed). But Laban tricked Jacob into marrying his older daughter, Leah, first. Jacob ended up working another seven years for Rachel, but "he also loved Rachel more than Le'ah," and "*ADONAI* saw that Le'ah was unloved" (29:30–31). Leah and Rachel became rivals for Jacob's love and favor, which he granted in the same limited way he experienced growing up. The sisters' competition for favor played out in the birth of Jacob's twelve sons. The sons kept the rivalry going among themselves, specifically uniting as the sons of the "hated" Leah, and of the two concubines as well, against Joseph, son of the "loved" Rachel. She will have one more son, Benjamin, and die in childbirth.

So Jacob projects his own identity struggle onto his marriage to the two sisters, and then onto Joseph and his brothers. Since Jacob received an insufficient dose of favor from his father, he's going to overcompensate with his chosen wife and her son and pile on the favor. After Rachel dies a tragic and early death, this compensatory move intensifies. It's not enough for him to love Joseph more than his brothers; he has to make that special love evident to anyone who might observe the family, and especially to Joseph's brothers. Jacob's *favor* might be a common-enough aspect of parenting, but his *favoritism* arises out of the pain of his early years, and he carries that pain into a new generation. From a family-dynamics perspective, it's unlikely that Jacob did any of this consciously. He probably didn't recognize the extent of his own favoritism toward Joseph. As we'll see shortly, Jacob seemed to be aware of the brothers' resentment, but didn't really address it, and even took actions bound to intensify it. Perhaps Jacob was so accustomed to tensions over favor from his own upbringing that he hardly noticed these tensions as they developed among his sons.

Joseph, following Jacob's lead, wears the garment of favor as a robe of status. This is the great temptation of those who receive favor—to see it as a status symbol, something to flaunt before those who don't receive it. This temptation works its way into our families, congregations and communities to this day. It's the source of tension and discord within these groups, and it's also one reason many people today don't want anything to do with "organized religion." Religious people often distort their sense of being blessed or favored by God into an issue of status.

In this way, Joseph flaunts his privilege in his brothers' faces. Some readers see Joseph as innocent, even flawless, a born hero, rather than a character who makes mistakes and learns from them to *become* a hero through many trials. But it's hard to see the young Joseph as virtuous or innocent in the way he relates to his brothers. His father's favor has gone to his head. He has two dreams of domination and just has to tell his whole family about them.

> "We were tying up bundles of wheat in the field when suddenly my bundle got up by itself and stood upright; then your bundles came, gathered around mine and prostrated themselves before it." His brothers retorted, "Yes, you will certainly be our king. You'll do a great job of bossing us around!" And they hated him still more for his dreams and for what he said.
>
> He had another dream which he told his brothers: "Here, I had another dream, and there were the sun, the moon and eleven stars prostrating themselves before me." He told his father too, as well as his brothers, but his father rebuked him: "What is this dream you have had? Do you really expect me, your mother and your brothers to come and prostrate ourselves before you on the ground?" His brothers were jealous of him, but his father kept the matter in mind. (37:7–11)

Jacob's favoritism leads him to overlook the arrogance, or at least indiscretion, Joseph displays by gloating over his dreams. He gives a mild rebuke, but instead of toning down his preference for Joseph, he soon sends him to check up on his brothers again and "bring me back word" (37:14). As he goes off to find his brothers, Joseph has a good distance to travel through the rugged open country of the land of Canaan, but nevertheless he wears his fancy *ketonet passim*. Apparently he just can't let it go. And so "they spotted him in the distance," because they can see his noble tunic from far off, before he's close enough for them to make out his features.

> And before he had arrived where they were, they had already plotted to kill him. They said to each other, "Look, this dreamer is coming! So come now, let's kill him and throw him into one of these water cisterns here. Then we'll say some wild animal devoured him. We'll see then what becomes of his dreams!" (37:18–20)

Reuben, the oldest brother, suggests they throw Joseph into the pit without killing him, hoping to save Joseph (and probably also to improve his standing as the official firstborn). Reuben's plan fails, but his goal of restoring Joseph to his father (37:22) reminds us that the brothers' crime isn't just against Joseph; it's also against their father. In rejecting Joseph the chosen, they reject Jacob the chooser. When they cast Joseph into the pit, they cast their own father into a pit of grief where he will languish, refusing to be comforted, for 22 years.

## A God who chooses

This intra-family dynamic hints at a major theme of Scripture we should explore briefly before we continue with our story: The God of Israel is a personal God who has the right to choose a person or tribe for his own reasons. Some modern readers see this idea as a real problem, leading to exclusivism, prejudice and violence.

> A truly rational and universal God, it is maintained, could not do anything so arbitrary as to "choose" one particular group out of mankind as a whole. . . . God is the God of all alike, and, therefore, cannot make distinctions between nations and peoples. To this is added the moral argument that the doctrine of "chosenness" is little better than crude ethnocentrism, in which a particular group regards itself as the center of the universe and develops doctrines that will flatter it pride and minister to its glory.[2]

Jewish thinker Will Herberg penned this analysis sixty years ago, and it would apply even more today, when the very idea of a chosen people, the very belief in a God who would choose one person or one nation, or even one religion, over another is scandalous. But to those who seek to read the Bible on its own terms, this idea—countercultural as it may be—is not only undeniably present, but an essential part of the whole biblical revelation. As one Christian reference notes, "The scriptural doctrine of divine capacity for choice demonstrates that purpose and personality, not blind mechanism, are at the heart of the universe." Jewish theologian Michael Wyschogrod ties this "divine capacity for choice" to God's nature as father:

> As a father, God loves his children and knows each one as who he is with his strengths and weaknesses, his virtues and vices. Because a father is not an impartial judge but a loving parent and because a human father is a human being with his own personality, it is inevitable that he will find himself more compatible with some of his children than others and, to speak very plainly, that he love some more than others.[3]

We might find this aspect of God's fatherhood troubling, because in choosing one child, God in some sense doesn't choose the rest. Wyschogrod addresses this concern:

> And it is also true that a father loves all his children, so that they all know of and feel the love they receive, recognizing that to substitute an impartial judge for a loving father would eliminate the preference for the specially favored but would also deprive all of them of a father.[4]

This particular-yet-universal love of God will be expressed in the theme of boundless favor that lies beneath the surface story of Joseph and his brothers.

Those who reject God's chosen ones risk rejecting God himself, whether they recognize it or not. This truth comes out most clearly in Exodus, where the Lord battles with Pharaoh over "my son, my firstborn, Israel" (4:22, literal translation). Pharaoh can only be saved if he'll recognize and honor God's choice of Israel, which of course he'll never do. Significantly, Joseph ends up in Egypt after his brothers betray him, setting the stage for the Exodus battle over Israel's chosenness that will come to a head several generations later.

## The bloody tunic

As we return to Joseph's story, the brothers are ready to throw him into the pit, but first they "stripped him of his tunic, the noble tunic that he was wearing" (37:23, literal translation). The Narrator is drawing our attention to this tunic, naming it twice in one phrase, then underlining its importance with words that would ordinarily be redundant: "that he was wearing." Of course he's wearing the tunic! What else would he be doing with it? But the Narrator is telling us, "Keep your eyes on this tunic."

By stripping Joseph of his tunic, the brothers are rejecting and defying the choice of their father. When they throw Joseph into the pit, they close their ears to his terrified cries for mercy (42:21)—and close their hearts to the unbearable suffering they're about to bring down on their father. They seem happy to torment Joseph, and even take a break for a snack in the process, but they're going to end up tormenting their father as well. After they toss Joseph in the pit, the brothers decide that instead of killing him, they'll sell him to some traders and trick his father—their father—into thinking he's been killed, an act nearly as bad as the murder they've avoided.

As this plot unfolds, Joseph's tunic makes a final appearance.

> Then they took Joseph's *tunic*, slaughtered a kid, and dipped the *tunic* in the blood. They had the *ornamented tunic* taken to their father, and they said, "We found this. Please examine it; is it your son's *tunic* or not?" He recognized it, and said, "My son's *tunic*! A savage beast devoured him! Joseph was torn by a beast!" (JPS TANAKH 37:31–33, emphasis added)

The Narrator repeats the word "tunic" five times in this brief passage to show us its central role as the symbol of favor. By stripping the tunic from Joseph and defiling it with blood, the brothers are subconsciously trying to undo the favor that's been given him. They view favor as a symbol of status, status that can be destroyed by removing a garment. Another dynamic is at play here as well. The brothers' words to their father are abrupt and harsh—"We found this. Please examine it; is it your son's tunic or not?" There's a modicum of politeness in the word "Please" (*Na* in Hebrew); beyond that the words are stark and comfortless, especially "your son" instead of "our brother" or even "Joseph" (as if they don't even want to name him), and the final phrase, "is it his or not?" Jacob's response is boundless grief: "'It's my son's robe! Some wild animal has torn Yosef in pieces and eaten him!' Ya'akov tore his clothes and, putting sackcloth around his waist, mourned his son for many days" (37:33–34). His family gathers around to comfort him, but he refuses to be comforted, for twenty-two years . . . and they refuse to uncover the secret that Joseph still lives. When the brothers reject Joseph as the favored one, they also reject their father's right to favor. They clearly get even with their brother for his arrogance and insensitivity, but they also reveal the depths of their resentment against their father.

## The triangle: Jacob, Joseph, the brothers

This scene is filled with tension, and the Midrash picks up on it. When the brothers ask Jacob if he recognizes his son's tunic, the Narrator says literally, "And he [Jacob] knew it, and said: It is my son's tunic." The Midrash paraphrases, "Said he to Judah: 'I know what a father sees'" (*Genesis Rabbah* 84.19). In this reading, Jacob is hinting that as father, he sees something going on among his sons beyond the obvious. I've always imagined the brothers bringing a torn, bloody tunic to their father, but the actual account here says nothing about it being torn—a lack that's especially striking since Reuben tears his clothes in 37:29 and Jacob tears his in 37:34.[5] Furthermore, Jacob's response to the bloody tunic is *Tarof, tarof Yosef*, literally, "Torn, torn is Joseph."[6] Joseph is torn, but apparently his tunic isn't. It's bloody, but no other sign of attack or foul play is upon it. Perhaps this tips off Jacob that something is going on behind the scenes. The Midrash notes that in the next chapter Judah will be comforted after his wife's death (38:12), but here Jacob refuses to be comforted (37:35). And so, when someone asks one of the rabbis of the

Midrash why that is, he responds, "You can be comforted for the
dead, but not for the living" (*Genesis Rabbah* 84:21).

A modern rabbi, Edwin Goldberg, adds another reason, along
with the suspect tunic, that Jacob might have believed Joseph
was still alive. When Joseph told his family about his dreams of
preeminence among them, "His brothers were jealous of him, but
his father kept the matter in mind" (37:11). Goldberg comments,

> If Jacob truly believes in the predictions of Joseph,
> then he has no choice but to conclude that Joseph still
> lives. Nevertheless, his suspicion of his remaining
> sons' sincerity leads him to play the role of a grieving
> father. Perhaps he intuits that his role is to act *as if* he
> believes them.[7]

The idea that Jacob suspects Joseph is still alive is admittedly a
stretch. Midrash, however, will often employ highly creative
interpretations to reveal profound insights, as I describe above.

In addition, the Midrash notes three players in this family
drama—Jacob, the brothers, and the absent Joseph—and the
brothers' treatment of Joseph is a case of triangulation. This is a
common family dynamic, which occurs, for example, when
"each parent demands that the child side with him against the
other parent."[8] A husband and wife have a conflict, perhaps over
his heavy drinking or her self-righteous nagging. Instead of
working out the conflict one-on-one, the wife draws in her oldest
son as an ally against the father. The conflict, tough enough to
begin with, becomes *triangulated*, and even harder to work out,
with the involvement of a third party, the child. Conversely,
triangulation can happen when parents who have never faced
their own differences make a child the scapegoat, the "bad kid"
who becomes the center of attention for the whole family.
Sometimes the "bad kid" is the one who creates the triangle

(unconsciously) by acting up to drive the parents closer together. The parents unite to deal with him, shifting their attention away from their own conflict, which can be terrifying to the child.

Another form of triangulation occurs when an adult with unresolved parental issues (which seems to include most of humankind) projects those issues onto a communal leader or mentor. This seems to be what's going on with Jacob and the brothers. The brothers resent Jacob's favoritism, and direct all of their resentment toward Joseph—which succeeds in indirectly punishing Jacob as well. In churches and synagogues, this triangulation can occur when an adult projects such parental issues onto the pastor or rabbi. I believe congregation is the human institution that is most like family, and issues carried over from family life often become reactivated in the life of the congregation. The spiritual leader is a father (or mother) figure, who might become subject to triangulation as a member works out old conflicts with a parent through him or her.

Triangulation doesn't occur simply by having a three-party, or triangular, relationship. From the perspective of Genesis 2, every marriage is triangular because every marriage has three parties—a man, a woman, and God who brings them together.

> The rib which *ADONAI*, God, had taken from the person, he made a woman-person; and he brought her to the man-person. . . . This is why a man is to leave his father and mother and stick with his wife, and they are to be one flesh. (Gen. 2:22, 24)

Because the triangle is the most stable geometric form, humans tend to relate to each other in a network of triangles: mother, father, child; husband, wife, in-law(s); two friends and a noble cause; members, rabbi, and a shared vision or problem or dogma. The primal marriage of Genesis 2 illustrates the most stable

triangular relationship, which is two individuals and God.
"Triangle formation is natural. Triangulation is another matter."[9]
A triangular relationship can be perfectly healthy in itself.
*Triangulation*, however, happens when issues between two parties
are projected onto the third party, or when a third party is brought
in, or steps in, to protect or control one of the two parties.

The power of triangulation—for good or ill—is that it allows
someone to redirect energy away from a difficult relationship to
one that seems more manageable, or to develop an ally to help
manage the difficult relationship. It seems to provide a measure
of control over a scary or unsatisfying relationship, but in the end
it often makes the problems worse.

The triangle here is between Joseph the chosen one, the non-
chosen brothers, and Jacob the chooser. At times the *ketonet
passim* itself forms a side of the triangle, so it becomes Joseph's
noble tunic, the non-chosen brothers, and Jacob the chooser. The
brothers have plenty of resentment toward their father, but in
their world there's no safe way to express it. So they make one of
triangulation's most common moves and create a scapegoat—
one who will bear the weight of the unresolved conflict between
two others. The brothers resent Joseph directly, but they also put
the weight of their resentment against Jacob on him as a
scapegoat. Then, when Joseph is out of the picture, they
scapegoat Joseph's tunic, enacting their jealousy and rage upon
it, and delivering it to their father, a token of the rage they feel
against him. Jacob seems to be aware of this triangulation and,
the Midrash imagines, also aware of the brothers' murderous
jealousy. He doesn't accept that Joseph has been torn by a beast,
but "knows what a father sees."

Triangulation doesn't always end by eliminating one of the
sides of the triangle. You can't get rid of Joseph, Jacob might be
telling his brothers, just by sending him away. Indeed, even if

Joseph is dead, he still forms a side of the triangle. The brothers will have to work out their relationship with their father with Joseph's favored status still in place, even if he is no more— another reason why Jacob refuses to be comforted.

When the Midrash has Jacob telling Judah, "I know what a father sees," it reminds us this is still Jacob's story. Most of the action swirls around Joseph and his brothers, but Jacob remains at the center. The whole *parasha* opened: "Ya'akov continued living in the land where his father had lived as a foreigner, the land of Kena'an. Here is the history of Ya'akov" (37:1–2). It's Jacob's story, and Jacob will not only remain engaged until the story reaches its climax and resolution, but will be at the center of the story throughout, whether physically present or not.

Nevertheless, if we take the Midrash seriously here, we still have to ask why Jacob wouldn't try to find Joseph, perhaps to even rescue him, if he believes he's still alive. Why would Jacob remain silent in the face of his sons' betrayal and his favored son's exile from the family? Why, as Rabbi Goldberg suggests, would he intuit "that his role is to act *as if* he believes them"— when acting this way does nothing to relieve Joseph's suffering?

This question gives rise to another one. Jacob had to know Joseph's brothers were jealous of him. He himself had rebuked Joseph for recounting his dreams of dominance so openly before them. When Jacob sent him out to find his brothers, he might have even noticed he was wearing his fancy tunic, which could only further stir up the brothers' resentment. Why would Jacob expose Joseph to his brothers' dangerous jealousy in the first place? Yes, this is all part of God's design, but it's also part of the irrational dynamics of family life. Jacob might have been in denial about the brothers' hatred for Joseph. He might have been so lost in his own favoritism that he didn't see what was going on. Or he might have unconsciously exposed Joseph to danger because it was somehow necessary for Joseph's identity formation, his hero's journey to adulthood, and Jacob may have sensed he wasn't to intervene.

## The silence of Jacob

The silence of the father is essential to understanding the theme of favor in Scripture, and how it works in human relationships as well. As a rabbi, I'm sometimes asked, "If the descendants of Jacob/Israel, the Jewish people, are really the Chosen People, why has their journey through history been so difficult?" Why has God—the Father who has chosen them—remained silent through the times of forced conversions, the burning and pillage of synagogues, the pogroms and Holocaust of modern times?

God, the chooser, doesn't necessarily protect his chosen ones from suffering. Indeed, in story after story, it seems the favored one has to endure suffering to fulfill his calling. Abraham must leave his native land and later offer up his beloved Isaac; Isaac must endure the deception of his son Jacob and his own wife, Rebekah; Jacob must experience a long and difficult exile. Toward the end of his days, Jacob will tell Pharaoh, "Few and hard have been the years of my life" (47:9). The suffering of the elect is vital to God's purposes for them—purposes that in the end benefit the non-elect as well. God must often remain silent in the midst of this suffering.

*The Chosen*, a novel by Chaim Potok, brings this theme to life in a modern family setting. It's the story of two young Jewish friends, Danny and Reuven, and their fathers. Danny's father, Reb Saunders, is a Hasidic *tzaddik* or holy man, a dynastic rabbi who is preparing his son to eventually take his mantle. When the boys first become friends, Danny tells Reuven that his father doesn't talk with him. Reuven comments on a month he spent with Danny's family.

> During the entire month I spent in Reb Saunders' house, the only time I ever saw him talk with Danny was when we argued over the Talmud. There was never any simple, intimate, human kind of conversation between him and his son. I almost had the impression that they were physically incapable of communicating with each other about ordinary things. (195)

Only at the end of the story does Reuven learn the reason for this excruciating silence. His friend Danny is the chosen one, who is to become a *tzaddik* like his father. It's evident from a very early age that Danny is also exceptionally brilliant—"a boy with a mind like a jewel," his father says. "There was no soul in my four-year-old Daniel, there was only his mind" (276-277). Reb Saunders' silence is his way of letting his beloved son go through what he must go through to develop the soul he must have to be a true chosen one. Pain, cultivated by silence, is an essential teacher, Reb Saunders explains.

> It destroys our self-pride, our arrogance, our indifference toward others. It makes us aware of how frail and tiny we are and of how much we must depend upon the Master of the Universe. (278)

At the end of the story, Danny chooses not to become a *tzaddik* in his father's footsteps, but to seek his own calling in life. He decides to study clinical psychology at Columbia University, which for him means shaving off his Hasidic beard and earlocks. Reuven asks Danny how his father reacted when he saw him without them.

He smiled sadly. "He's not happy about it. He said he almost doesn't recognize me."

"He talked to you?"

"Yes," Danny said quietly. "We talk now." (284)

Now that Danny is no longer Reb Saunders' heir, he begins to have a normal father-son relationship with him. The young Daniel Saunders reminds me of young Joseph, who is gifted, charismatic, but lacking in soul. He's ready to bring a bad report about his brothers, ready to describe in detail his dreams of domination, without awareness of how such actions might affect others. Perhaps Jacob's silence regarding Joseph's suffering, whether a literal part of the story or an imaginative flight based upon it, is essential for Joseph specifically because he is so favored.

## The hero's painful journey

Jacob remains silent, not intervening in the events that will form Joseph's soul according to God's design. To put this another way, Jacob understands Joseph must take a hero's journey to become the person he is meant to be. As I noted in the Introduction, the hero's journey takes him or her away from family and homeland—and even into the trials and suffering of exile—before it can bring the hero back home transformed and empowered. Jacob as a father might want to protect his son from such a journey, but he senses he cannot.

Family therapist Rabbi Edwin Friedman employs a term that captures the dual meaning of identity formation: differentiation, "the capacity to be an 'I' while remaining connected."[10] The capacity to be an "I" might sound like the typical self-centered and individualistic jargon of our day, so Rabbi Friedman makes it clear that remaining connected, remaining part of the family, is essential to differentiation. He insists, "The concept should not be confused with autonomy or narcissism" (two very popular dysfunctions of our day). Joseph could have chosen the route of autonomy, seeing his experience of betrayal as setting him free from his hung-up, dysfunctional family to become his own man. His hero's journey would have had a one-way route, and he'd leave, never to return, and never to resolve his relationship with the family. Or he could have taken the path of narcissism, which seemed to tempt him in his early years—a path so much about him that no one else mattered at all.

But both these options represent a spiritual dead-end, and differentiation as Rabbi Friedman describes it provides a better way forward. It's a way that reflects the hero's journey, which departs from home and family, endures trials and transformation, but returns in the end. Such a journey is difficult, particularly for the offspring of a great parent, like Jacob. The son or daughter looks at a talented, powerful or charismatic parent and despairs of being able to follow that act with one of their own. It's also difficult for the offspring of particularly troubled or needy parents, who might feel they need to stick around to keep things from falling apart, or who might lack the confidence to set out on their own. Either situation can lead to a failure to journey at all, so that the new generation just rests on the old generation's laurels, or lives in its gloomy shadow, and never makes its own mark. Or the hero can take a one-way journey, seeking to find him or herself by rebelling, refusing to cooperate, or breaking with the family altogether. As Rabbi Friedman points out, however, this sort of journey doesn't lead to genuine differentiation, because the disconnected offspring is still defining himself or herself in contrast with the family, instead of as a distinct "I" who remains connected.

Friedman writes that differentiation is an essential task for every leader. Peter Steinke provides a fuller description of differentiation, which can help us with leadership in our families as well as congregations:

> Differentiation is the relative ability of people to guide their own functioning by
>
> ▸ thinking clearly
>
> ▸ acting on principle
>
> ▸ defining self by taking a position
>
> ▸ coming to know more about their own instinctive reactions to others
>
> ▸ learning to regulate those reactions
>
> ▸ staying in contact with others
>
> ▸ choosing a responsible course of action
>
> Differentiation is . . . about balancing two life forces—individuality and togetherness—when interacting with others.[11]

Joseph, a uniquely gifted leader, is favored as soon as his story gets underway, but he can't find himself and fulfill his mission until he takes his long journey of differentiation. Only after years on his journey can he become not just his father's favorite, but his own man, who remains dedicated to his father and his father's God. Perhaps Jacob knows Joseph's descent into Egypt is the only route to such differentiation. Sometimes the wise parent fosters differentiation by not intervening, by knowing when to allow sons or daughters to strike out on their own, by even blessing their departure, painful as it is.

# Judah and Tamar

After Joseph is sold into slavery in Egypt, the Narrator leads us on what appears to be a detour, recounting the tale of Joseph's brother Judah and his daughter-in-law Tamar. [12] In reality, though, Judah's story is no detour. It is essential to the larger tale of Jacob's sons. Reuben, the firstborn, had already disqualified himself as Jacob's heir when he "went and slept with Bilhah his father's concubine" (35:22; 49:3–4). Simeon and Levi would have been next in line, but they proved themselves unworthy by their treacherous and violent behavior toward Shechem (34; 49:5). Now the action shifts to Judah, who follows Simeon and Levi in birth order. He is in place to head the family, and we'll see some evidence that he wants to, but will he prove himself worthy to be Jacob's heir?

This question brings out a tension within the whole story— actually, *two* sources of tension. First is the tension between Judah and Joseph over who is to be Jacob's chosen heir. Joseph seems on track for that role, but he is diverted to Egypt, and then the focus shifts to Judah. Which one will ultimately emerge as the heir?

The other source of tension is the ambiguity over *why* God favors one over the other. Is his choice simply up to him, independent of any human actions, good or bad? This seemed to be the case with Jacob and Esau. Before they were even *born*, before they had done anything good or bad, the Lord told Rebekah their mother, "the older [Esau] shall serve the younger [Jacob]", thus overturning the normal status of the firstborn (25:23; see Rom. 9:10–13). On the other hand, there is also the sense that God chooses the one who deserves it most, as seemed to be the case with Cain and Abel (4:3–5). Cain brought an offering; Abel brought the choicest of his firstlings. The offering represented Abel's deep devotion to God, so he was favored and Cain was not. Understood in this way, this story reflects the sort of choice in which God favors the one who has already shown that he deserves it.

Judah's story seems to fall into this second category. Jacob has already chosen Joseph, but perhaps Judah, the eldest son who hasn't already disqualified himself, is the one who deserved to be chosen. This issue comes into sharper focus when we recall that Joseph is taken out of the picture for twenty-plus years. Perhaps Jacob believes that Joseph is still alive, as one Midrash suggests, but he doesn't—or can't—do anything about it. Whether dead or only missing, the heir that he chose is out of the picture, so who will be heir in his place? Is Judah worthy? The drama of favor has become even more complex, and the story of Judah and Tamar belongs right here in the middle of the drama for this reason.

This part of Judah's story opens with ironic contrast. Joseph is taken *down* to Egypt (37:25, 39:1) and sold to Potiphar, then "it happened at this time that Judah went *down* from his brothers" (38:1, emphasis added). Joseph descends against his will, Judah deliberately; but both must descend into trials and humiliation to reach God's objective. Joseph's descent to Egypt was necessary for his differentiation, the process of becoming his own man but remaining connected to his family (though with a 22-year interlude). Judah also goes down, and the Narrator explicitly says he goes down from his brothers, thus beginning to differentiate himself. But just going off to become your own man is no great accomplishment. We'll see as the story progresses how Judah remains connected with his family in a way that's absolutely essential for their restoration.

Without this context, Judah's story does seem like an interruption, as many commentators claim.[13] It comes between

"And the Midianites sold him [Joseph] into Egypt" (37:36) and "Joseph was brought down to Egypt" (39:1). The Midrash says this apparent interruption "was done in order to bring two passages of 'descent' together" (*Genesis Rabbah* 85:2). The Midrash focuses on the one word, "descent," that connects the two stories, but they are connected in a broader way as well. Joseph and Judah both have a claim to be the firstborn. Joseph is favored by his father and will become God's vessel for saving the entire family of Israel. Judah is the oldest son to remain qualified as heir, and he will be the one to take the decisive step that allows the family of Israel to be made whole, as we'll see later. By placing Judah's story immediately after the opening of Joseph's, Genesis indicates that the story of favor is really about both of them.

Furthermore, the theme of descent isn't just an interesting coincidence between the two stories; it is essential to both, and to our understanding of God's favor. Suffering is an inherent part of being chosen. Every chosen one in Scripture endures suffering on the way to fulfilling God's purpose. Bad things happen to people of faith, people with a claim to God's favor, just as they do to everyone else. What changes is the *meaning* of those bad things—they are not random defeats and disappointments, but stages on the hero's journey, stages *every* favored one must traverse.

So, after Judah goes down from his brothers, he marries, and eventually fathers three sons. The oldest son, Er, takes a wife named Tamar, but he "was evil from *ADONAI*'s perspective, so *ADONAI* killed him" (38:7). The second son, Onan, according to the custom of the time, marries Tamar in order to raise up offspring for his brother, but refuses to fulfill this responsibility and likewise dies because of his evil. Judah withholds his youngest son, Shelah, from Tamar because he's afraid he also will end up dead. Eventually, Judah's wife dies, and he goes up to Timnah, where he keeps his flocks, to oversee their shearing. Tamar disguises herself as a harlot and goes out to sit alongside the road to Timnah, "For she saw that Shelah had grown up, but she still was not being given to him as his wife" (38:14). When the lonely and unsuspecting Judah comes down the road, she induces him to lie with her, after they agree on the price of a kid from his flock. Judah cannot pay at the time, so he gives his signet, cord and staff as a pledge, in place of the kid, to Tamar, whom he still doesn't recognize (38:18). The seal, attached to a cord and worn around the neck, "was a highly personal object that performed the function of the signature in modern society, a kind of extension of the personality. Judah leaves part of himself with Tamar when he gives her his seal."[14] Likewise, the staff is part of Judah's attire and a symbol of his status and power.

Tamar takes all these items from Judah to guarantee he will send her the payment of a prostitute. Then they lie together and Tamar conceives. She keeps all this a secret until she is found to be pregnant. When Judah hears about Tamar's pregnancy, his response is shocking: "Bring her out, and let her be burned alive!" (38:24). It's hard not to suspect that Judah sees an opportunity to get rid of Tamar, whom he blames for the death of his two sons and sees as a threat to the life of his third. But Tamar is prepared. As she's being led off to execution, she produces Judah's seal, cord and staff, and cries out,

> "I am pregnant by the man to whom these things belong. Determine, I beg you, whose these are—the signet, the cords and the staff." Then Y'hudah acknowledged owning them. He said, "She is more righteous than I, because I didn't let her become the wife of my son Shela." (38:25–26)

Judah has to acknowledge in public that the pledged items belong to him. This humiliation awakens him to the sin he committed against Tamar by withholding his son from her, and her innocence: "She is more righteous than I."

As we've seen, the Midrash notes parallels between this story and Joseph's story. The first parallel is that both brothers descend, or go down. Here's a second parallel—"Rabbi Johanan said: In order to bring the two phrases, 'Discern, I pray thee' together" (*Genesis Rabbah* 85:2). The first time we hear this phrase is when Joseph's brothers bring Joseph's bloodied tunic to Jacob, saying, "We found this. *Discern, I pray thee*; is it thy son's tunic or not?" (37:32, my translation) The brothers are trying to deceive their father with a garment. One of the Hebrew words for "garment," *beged*, is related to the word *bagad*, which means to betray or act treacherously.[15] A garment normally corresponds to the status or inner quality of a person, as David's daughter Tamar realized when she had to tear the garment that signified her virginity. But a garment can also be used to misrepresent or deny the inner quality. The brothers send the bloody garment to their father to deceive him into thinking Joseph is dead. Jacob, of course, had also used a garment to deceive his father many years earlier, when he wore Esau's *beged* at his mother Rebekah's urging, to trick Isaac into giving him the blessing Isaac really wanted to give to Esau (27:15, 27:27). This supports the idea that Jacob suspected Joseph was still alive after the brothers brought him the bloody garment. One who employs a trick to deceive someone isn't going to fall for the same sort of trick himself!

This legacy of deception reminds us that transgressions travel from generation to generation, and the behavior of children reiterates, sometimes tragically, the parents' behavior. The 21st-century narrative might tell us we're born as free and independent creatures, able to make of our lives anything we set our minds to. Scripture, and reality itself, reveal a darker picture. The sins of the fathers are visited upon the children to the third and fourth generation of those alienated from God (Ex. 20:5; 34:7), but God is "merciful and compassionate, slow to anger, rich in grace and truth" (Ex. 34:6), and he provides a way to break out of this pattern through repentance and redemption, as we'll see.

Now, Tamar uses garments to deceive Judah, who had joined his brothers in deceiving Jacob with a garment. She takes off the garments of widowhood and puts on the veil of a harlot. When Judah sees her, he thinks she is a harlot because she covered her face (38:14–15). Later, Tamar produces Judah's signet, cord and staff to prove he is the father of the child she is bearing. Just as the brothers had sent word to Jacob, Tamar sends word to Judah, *"Discern I pray thee* to whom these belong"—the second appearance of this phrase in the story of Joseph and his brothers. Tamar used clothing to deceive Judah into lying with her, and now she uses clothing (or accessories) to "deceive" Judah into acknowledging his wrong: "She is more righteous than I, because I didn't let her become the wife of my son Shela" (38:26).

## Judah's repentance

Judah's descent also means, according to one midrash, that "his status falls, because his brothers blame him for the selling of Yosef and the distress of Ya'akov."[16] In this view, Judah was the ringleader of the evil plot against Joseph, which shattered the family of Israel, but he will emerge as the brother who eventually does what it takes to make his family whole. When Tamar deceives Judah with the garments of a prostitute, it's as if she's telling him he deceives himself with his garments of status. He thinks he's a big shot, despite his failings, and this attitude shows up when he uses his status to condemn Tamar to death without mercy and without a hearing. But she reminds him of who he really is, stripped of the emblems of power, and he must admit, "She is more righteous than I."

Judah's repentance here provides a contrast between him and Joseph. Joseph seems pretty puffed up in his early years, but Judah is the one who has to repent. Joseph appears to be the innocent victim of his jealous brothers—but ironically, Judah's repentance hints that he's the one who will be chosen in the end. The sages used to say, "Better one hour of repentance and good deeds in this world than all the life in the World-to-Come."[17] Yeshua the Messiah said, "There will be more joy in heaven over one sinner who turns to God from his sins than over ninety-nine righteous people who have no need to repent" (Luke 15:7). Perhaps Judah's repentance—despite its sordid backdrop— prepares him to rise among his brothers in a way Joseph's innocence cannot. It foreshadows the turning-point of the whole story, which will depend on Judah's ability to finally recognize his wrongdoing toward Joseph and Jacob, turn away from it, and make real amends.

Furthermore, the point of Judah's repentance in Genesis 38 isn't just that he has sinned and needs God's forgiveness. The nature of the sin is vital to the story, because it involves procreation, one of the main themes of Genesis. Judah's second son, Onan, is destroyed because he refuses to contribute his seed to the line of his older brother Er. Judah commits the same transgression because he refuses to contribute his seed, that is, his youngest son Shelah. He has to be tricked into providing seed for Tamar.

Symbolically, in withholding Shelah, Judah sins—just
like Onan—against Tamar, against his eldest son, and
also against his entire family and the law-abiding
community. He defies the commandment to be fruitful
and multiply, he denies Tamar her marital and maternal
fulfillment, he neglects the duty (Shelah's) to be one's
brother's keeper, and he prefers the love of his own to the
keeping of the law.[18]

Therefore, when Judah acknowledges Tamar's righteousness and
his own failure, he is showing deep repentance. He is
acknowledging the priority of God's agenda, of preserving the
family line and protecting the wholeness of the family, even at
the expense of his own preferences. This is the exact issue
Joseph will raise later when his brothers come down to Egypt—
will they choose the wholeness of the family over their own
priorities and comfort? It's a choice that's especially relevant
today, when the individual and his/her dreams and goals are
exalted, and the family is often seen as an impediment. That
portrayal of things looks exciting, especially to young people just
starting out on their own, but it ignores the loneliness and
isolation, and the burden of unresolved issues, which often ensue
when we try to leave our families totally behind.

Judah repents of that sort of self-motivated action and is now
prepared to do the right thing when the big test for his family
comes. In the meantime, through her union with Judah, Tamar
bears twins, one of whom becomes an ancestor of King David,
and therefore of the Messiah. On the opening words of Genesis
38, "And it came to pass at that time," the Midrash says, "The
tribal ancestors were engaged in selling Joseph, Jacob was taken
up with his sackcloth and fasting [in grief over Joseph], and
Judah was busy taking a wife, while the Holy One, blessed be

He, was creating the light of Messiah," through the union of Judah and Tamar (*Genesis Rabbah* 85.1). Joseph descends into Egypt and his father descends into grief. Judah descends from his brothers to find a wife, and ends up inaugurating the line of Messiah, whose light will rise upon Israel.

The birth of the twins Peretz and Zerach re-enacts our theme of sibling rivalry (38:27–30). Zerach makes a claim at being first-born by sticking his hand out of the womb. The midwife marks it by tying a scarlet thread on it, but Peretz pushes through to be born first, as his name, which means "breaking out," signifies.

> This triumph-of-the-younger-son motif thus looks back to the struggle between Jacob and Esau, but more immediately to Joseph's dreams, in which he saw his brothers bowing down to him. The . . . reinforcement of this principle in chap. 38 is an assurance that Joseph's dreams will ultimately be fulfilled.[19]

Pushy Peretz, ancestor of Messiah, is born of incest and deception. Far from disqualifying Judah's line, however, this birth roots it in the common lot of humanity, so that it is fit to produce a Messiah who will represent all humankind. As I noted in the introduction, being chosen is a result or outcome of favor. Through God's favor, which is undeserved, the line of Peretz is chosen for the awesome assignment of bringing forth Messiah. And so we see that being chosen doesn't mean being deemed perfect, but being called forth in your imperfection by God's special mercy and kindness. Israel itself, as God's chosen people, doesn't claim perfection. Rather, Scripture reveals Israel's human fallibility, which paradoxically equips Israel to represent the rest of humankind and to bring forth the Messiah himself.

## The power of inherited narrative

Long before the story of Judah and Tamar reaches its climax, Joseph arrives in Egypt. As much as his story parallels Judah's, it even more closely aligns with that of his father Jacob. In Egypt, Joseph will endure exile and many trials before he is finally restored to his family and his destiny. In the same way, as a young man, Jacob was exiled from his land and family and had to endure many trials before he was able to return. Jacob lived with intense rivalry with his brother Esau, his uncle Laban, and between his wives, Leah and Rachel. Joseph lived with intense rivalry with his brothers. From our family-dynamics perspective, this father-son parallel is true not just of Jacob and Joseph, but of many, perhaps most, families. The family drama of one generation continues on in the next, and to understand the current generation, we need to look back at the lives of its parents and grandparents. Don't overlook the power of inherited narrative.

I once had a client I'll call Bob, a successful, highly respected physician in our city, who'd gotten hooked on opioids after undergoing back surgery.[20] Eventually he realized his drug abuse wasn't just about his physical pain, but had a life of its own, which now threatened his whole career and family, including the future of his three children, ages nine through fifteen. Bob stopped using, joined a good support group, and started individual counseling with me. As Bob started bringing his life back into focus, he recalled his early years living with an alcoholic father, who was considered a pillar of the community, but was a terror at home whenever he drank. Eventually Bob's father was fired from his job for arriving visibly drunk. He responded to his fall by going into recovery, and over the years sponsored a good number of other men who successfully renounced their drinking and established new lives for themselves and their families. Bob's drugging compulsively reenacted his father's life and revisited the trauma it caused Bob. But his recovery also drew on the legacy his father had created. As a therapist, I couldn't fully understand Bob apart from his father's story, which had become Bob's inherited narrative. Understanding the bigger story doesn't excuse or minimize the behavior that's so deeply intertwined with it, but it enables and enhances the recovery process. As you come to understand the inherited narrative more fully, it can be reshaped through repentance, forgiveness and the restoration of trust. As we continue our tale, we'll see Joseph reshaping, through forgiveness and restored trust, the narrative of zero-sum rivalry he inherited from Jacob.

Jacob's story helps us to understand Joseph's story, which grows out of it. As the Jewish commentators note, "The whole course of the son's life is but a repetition of the father's."[21] The most significant parallel is that, against a background of sibling rivalry and exile, both men experience unique favor. And both their stories reveal that being favored is no simple matter, and doesn't create a smooth path for the chosen one. The next leg of Joseph's journey makes that abundantly clear.

## Potiphar's wife

In Egypt, Joseph is sold to Potiphar, an officer of Pharaoh. There, Joseph prospers and is swiftly elevated, so that he has charge of the entire household. The first part of 39:6 summarizes, "So he [Potiphar] left all his possessions in Yosef's care; and because he had him, he paid no attention to his affairs, except for the food he ate." Then the verse abruptly changes its focus: "Now Yosef was well-built and handsome as well." The Narrator is using the identical Hebrew words he used to describe Rachel in Gen. 29:17. Joseph's father Jacob loves Rachel because she is "beautiful in form and appearance," and he serves patiently to win her as his bride. Potiphar's wife lusts after Joseph because he is "beautiful in form and appearance," and strives impatiently to seduce him. Finally, she loses patience, until one day,

> he came into the house to do his work. None of the household being there inside, she caught hold of him by *his garment* and said, "Lie with me!" But he left *his garment* in her hand and got away and fled outside. When she saw that he had left *his garment* in her hand and had fled outside, she called out to her servants and said to them, "Look, he had to bring us a Hebrew to dally with us! This one came to lie with me; but I screamed loud. And when he heard me screaming at the top of my voice, he left *his garment* with me and got away and fled outside." She kept *his garment* beside her, until his master came home. Then she told him the same story, saying, "The Hebrew slave whom you brought into our house came to me to dally with me; but when I screamed at the top of my voice, he left *his garment* with me and fled outside." (39:11–18 JPS TANAKH, emphasis added)

The phrase "his garment" is one word in Hebrew, *bigdo*. As always, when the Narrator repeats a word, he is drawing attention to it and trying to tell us something. In this eight-verse passage, *bigdo* appears six times.[22] That's a lot of repetition, but what exactly is it telling us? In the story of Tamar and Judah, Tamar uses garments to deceive Judah. She removes the (true) garment of widowhood to put on the deceptive garments of harlotry, then puts her true garments back on when the deception is accomplished. Likewise, Jacob's mother, Rebekah, had used Esau's garments to deceive Isaac into granting his blessing to Jacob instead of Esau (27:15–27). Now, in Potiphar's house, garments take a lead role again. Joseph isn't deceived by them, but he is framed by garments so that Potiphar is deceived and Joseph ends up in prison. As with Esau's garments of the field and Tamar's garments of widowhood, Joseph's garments become an instrument of deception, and it's a deception that in the end accomplishes God's purposes. On a human level, the act of deceiving another person is always wrong, but sometimes the outcome of such an act is right. God forbid that we should use this fact as an excuse for deception. The point is rather that God can make something good even of our failures and shortcomings.

The potential of garments to deceive reminds us that the family is the place, of all places, where we shouldn't try to deceive anyone. When we're at home, around our family members, we can just relax and wear whatever is handy and comfortable. We don't need to wear clothes that suggest status or enable us to play a particular role. We can just be ourselves, and be accepted . . . or so it should be. Genesis reveals, however, that even the family is touched by evil and corruption. We can't heal our families by reviving our lost innocence, just as we can't recreate the unashamed nakedness of Adam and Eve in the Garden of Eden. But Genesis also reveals the way of healing and restoration of our families, even if it's a long and demanding journey.

And so Joseph's journey completes the process that began with the removal of the garment of status, the *ketonet passim*. He is again deprived of a garment and sent further down and further away from his family. His descent just gets worse and worse, but it's essential to his eventual rise and to God's whole plan for him and his family. The path of the favored one takes devious turns. This reality doesn't justify or excuse deception, but it does reveal that God's purposes prevail even through human weakness and moral compromise.

## Joseph the number-two man

In Potiphar's house Joseph had risen quickly to preeminence so that he was soon Potiphar's chief servant, in charge of everything. Of course, Joseph's fall from favor in Potiphar's house was sudden too. But then he rises back up in prison, apparently very rapidly again. These two ascents have several features in common:

► Both begin at zero—Joseph starts out as a nameless and faceless slave, as property, not a person. He returns to that status in prison, as one among a number of the king's prisoners.

► In both cases, "the Lord was with Joseph" (39:2, 21) in a way that is undeniable to his Egyptian masters.

► In both cases the master looks positively upon Joseph because of this. "The LORD . . . gave him *favor* in the eyes of the ruler of the prison" (39:21, literal translation).

► Both masters—Potiphar and the chief jailer—soon turn everything over to Joseph.

► In both cases, the Lord gives Joseph great success.

Spoiler alert: Those familiar with Joseph's story know he will end up in the same position in Pharaoh's court—the number-two man who is so invested in the master's interests, and so capable, that the master can entrust everything to him and sit back to enjoy the results. When Joseph was a teenager he had begun to take a similar role in his father's house. Joseph is the perfect number-two man any father, court official or king would want by his side. His readiness to fully commit himself to the interests of his superior is evident in scene after scene of his saga.

From a family-systems perspective, however, such a role is generally *not* associated with the firstborn. Joseph receives the favor and status-marker that belong to the firstborn, and he is indeed the firstborn of his father's favorite wife, but in taking the role of right-hand man, he doesn't act like the typical firstborn. When we use the term "firstborn" today, we're just thinking of the first child born to a couple or a single parent. We're not thinking of a special, ceremonial or legal status, but simple birth-order. The chronologically firstborn child is often the one who most aggressively strikes out on his own, who makes his distinctive mark on the world. In the tales of Genesis, Ishmael and Esau are chronologically firstborn, and are both dynamic figures who leave the family fold to create their own place within the wider world, even if they become less significant in Israel's family story. As Rabbi Sacks points out, the firstborn is never the one chosen in the initial generations of Abraham's line, because the firstborn is *naturally* qualified.

> The choice of Isaac instead of Ishmael has many dimensions, but they all share one feature: they are a refusal to let nature have the final word. . . .
>
> Most fundamentally, Isaac has none of the attributes of a mythic hero. Unlike Ishmael, he is *not* strong, physical, at home in the fields and forests. The same contrast will later be played out by Esau and Jacob.[23]

Isaac remains with his father, and is obedient to him, even to the point of nearly letting his father kill him as a sacrifice. Jacob is "a quiet man who stayed in the tents" (25:27). Joseph as the favored son carries this trait of family loyalty to its greatest fulfillment. The literal firstborn in Genesis, on the other hand, seems unfit to advance the family legacy. Reuben, "my firstborn, my strength, the firstfruits of my manhood . . . superior in vigor and power," turns out to be "unstable as water" (49:3–4). Often the later-born son is more fit to fulfill the task of preserving and carrying forward the legacy of the family, because he is not intent on creating his own legacy. In Scripture, the chosen one is not what Rabbi Sacks calls a mythic hero, but one who plays a secondary role to the father, or like Joseph, to whatever master he is called to serve.

In my work with families, I've noticed it's not the firstborn, but often a later-born, or even the last-born, who is the golden boy or girl of the family. The firstborn launches out on his own, makes a mark on the world, but is so intent on making his own way that he loses close contact with the family. A younger son or daughter takes his place as the real or potential family hero, and often as the one who takes care of the aging parents as time goes on. I was recently talking with some members of a family that had been part of our congregation years earlier, when I was a local rabbi. The father had had a dramatic encounter with God a few years before they joined us. He had made a strong commitment to Yeshua and expected all his children to do the same. The older brothers had already left home and were having lots of ups and downs in life, but Ben, the youngest, was still there, showing a lot of promise and living like a true follower of Yeshua. As we were talking about this, Alan, one of the older brothers, grinned sheepishly and said, "Yeah, Ben was like Joseph, and our father pinned all his hopes on him." Sometimes it's not the firstborn, but the younger son who's the golden boy, and that's how it was with Joseph.

But before Joseph can enter the service of Pharaoh and get on with fulfilling God's whole plan for his life, he has to be delivered from prison himself. As our *parasha* comes to a close, the stage is set. Joseph has two fellow prisoners, the chief cupbearer and the chief baker of Pharaoh's court. Both have fallen out of favor with the king and both have a dream on the same night, "each dream with its own meaning" (40:5). Both men are downcast in the morning because they both sense their dreams mean something significant, but there's no one to tell them what it is. Joseph responds, "Don't interpretations belong to God? Tell it to me, please" (40:8b).

Just as a pair of dreams at the beginning of our story led to Joseph's downfall, now a pair of dreams will lead to his deliverance, and later a final pair of dreams will open the way to Joseph's true destiny. When Joseph told his brothers about his first set of dreams, he appeared to be exalting himself, and his father rebuked him. Now, when he offers to interpret this new set of dreams, it's not about him at all—it's not he but God who can interpret. Joseph is learning he's not at the center of the story, God is, and he's ready to say so. According to the God-given interpretation, then, Pharaoh will pardon and free the cupbearer, and have the chief baker cruelly executed. And so it comes to pass. But even though Joseph asks the cupbearer to put in a good word for him when he gets back to Pharaoh's court, the *parasha* ends, "Nevertheless, the chief cupbearer didn't remember Yosef, but forgot him" (Gen. 40:23).

# Chapter Two

# *Mikketz*
# "At the end"

*At the end of two years, Pharaoh had a dream.*

The forgetful cupbearer leaves Joseph languishing in prison. His deliverance must await this new *parasha*, which opens two years after the cupbearer was released, when Pharaoh has a twofold dream no one can interpret. At last, the cupbearer remembers Joseph, and tells Pharaoh about this young Hebrew and his amazing ability to interpret dreams. "Then Pharaoh summoned Yosef, and they brought him quickly out of the dungeon. He shaved himself, changed his clothes, and came in to Pharaoh" (41:14). It's not hard to imagine Joseph the dream-master now wondering if *he's* in a dream. He sheds his prison rags for a new set of clothes and steps out of the deep gloom of the dungeon into the glaring light of an Egyptian day. It's a moment of high drama, and as in the whole drama of Joseph and his brothers, the costumes themselves play a major role. This is the last of three critical scenes in which clothing, put on or taken off, is essential in preparing Joseph for his ultimate task. The first two scenes took place in our last *parasha*, Vayeshev, so let's backtrack a bit.

The first removal of Joseph's garments was at the hand of his brothers, when they took off his *ketonet passim*, dipped it in blood, and sent it to their father:

> He recognized it, and said, "My son's tunic! A savage beast devoured him! Joseph was torn by a beast!" Jacob rent his clothes, put sackcloth on his loins, and observed mourning for his son many days. (Gen. 37:33–34)

It's hard to miss the starring role of garments in this scene. The brothers deceive their father with Joseph's blood-stained garment. Jacob's response is to tear his garment, and then put on a new garment of sackcloth to gird himself for the long journey of mourning ahead of him. As we've seen, the torn garment is an ancient custom of mourning, still practiced by Jews today. The garment is damaged, to mark the one who wears it as damaged by grief, outside the normal flow of life's activities for a time, raw and incomplete.

The very first appearance of clothing in the Bible was the "tunics of skin" ("tunic" here is *ketonet*, as in Joseph's story), which God provided for Adam and Eve after their sin (Gen. 3:21). One commentator says, "Clothing, besides its obvious protective function, is one of the most pervasive of human symbols through which a person's position and role in society is signaled."[1] Clothing, in other words, displays identity—marking both where one belongs, and how one stands out within the group he or she belongs to. So in our tale, Jacob's torn garment, and the sackcloth he adds to it, displays his identity as a mourner, a member of the community who stands out because of his mourning. Joseph's fancy tunic displays his identity as a member of Jacob's family who stands out because of his favor. The significance of the two displays is nearly opposite: pride and status on one side; loss and grief on the other. A garment set off

Joseph's identity as the favored son, until his brothers stripped it from him. In time, garments will display a much deeper identity as favored one, an identity Joseph will gain through his long journey down to Egypt.

After his brothers sold Joseph down to Egypt, he quickly rose to prominence and caught the eye of the wife of Potiphar, his master. Joseph resisted her attempt to seduce him, so she grabbed his garment and he fled, leaving it in her hand. Potiphar's wife used the abandoned garment to deceive her husband into believing Joseph attacked her, and he was stripped of his position in Potiphar's house and cast into prison. The Lord had been with Joseph and blessed him in all he did, yet Joseph had to be stripped again of whatever status he had gained in Potiphar's house to reach his true destiny.

Finally, in our current *parasha*, when Joseph is summoned before Pharaoh, he has to lose his garment again, his prison garb, so he can stand before the great king. We can only imagine the stunning brightness of Joseph's deliverance. It's been two long years since the cupbearer was released from prison as Joseph had predicted, and nothing has happened. Joseph is still trusting the Lord and serving the prison keeper the best he can, but surely he must struggle with discouragement and even despair. Then, suddenly, out of nowhere, messengers from Pharaoh burst into his dark cell and tell him he's been summoned to appear before the king. But first, the garments: "He shaved himself, changed his clothes, and came in to Pharaoh" (Gen. 41:14b).

Once in Pharaoh's presence, Joseph provides an interpretation of his twofold dream that convinces all who hear it. Then he has the chutzpah to add some advice on how Pharaoh can avoid the disaster the dreams warn of. Pharaoh decides no one is better qualified than Joseph to lead the disaster relief, and he gives him full authority to do so, right on the spot—and signifies his decision with another change of garments. "Pharaoh said to Yosef, 'Here, I place you in charge of the whole land of Egypt.' Pharaoh took his signet ring off his hand and put it on Yosef's hand, had him clothed in fine linen with a gold chain around his neck" (41:41–42). Joseph's identity as the favored one is finally made visible again, but now, because of his long ordeal, he's prepared to bear the robe of status with a servant's attitude. He's raised up to deliver his people, along with Egypt and all the nations.

The yearning for favor, the yearning to receive a unique blessing and affirmation from the father or mother, is inherent to human nature, and is a driving force within human families. In our era of family breakdown, this yearning is often redirected to other sources of affirmation, like peers in childhood and adolescence, or teachers and supervisors later in life. But the drive remains, as does the calculus of comparison and competition. This transfer of yearning for parental affirmation to figures beyond the family is a contemporary reality, but it's already evident in the stories of Genesis as well. Abraham the exile, living as an undocumented alien in the land of promise, receives the blessing and affirmation of Melchizedek, a king of that land. Does Melchizedek replace the father Abraham left behind in Haran? Joseph, estranged from his father, serves Potiphar, the jailer, and finally Pharaoh, with the loyalty of a devoted son. Joseph's yearning for favor seems to transfer from the father to whoever is in authority. And that story is repeated for countless lost and orphaned sons and daughters in the centuries that follow.

Joseph's story reveals that this yearning for favor and the rivalry it inspires not only affects families, but is transferred into many different relational systems, as we see in today's culture. When the rivalry for favor is focused beyond siblings, it shows up in comparison and competition between peers, co-workers, even members of the same church or synagogue. Spiritual community is undermined by jockeying for power, status, or attention—sometimes subtle and sometimes all-too obvious. But Joseph's story will also point beyond such contested favor to a boundless favor that results in blessing to all the siblings—even if it entails suffering for the favored one. A complex but enlightening thread in the story will help us understand this particular dynamic of favor more fully.

## Messiah ben Joseph

Readers of Joseph's story throughout the ages have seen him as a type or symbol of another deliverer to come. Ramban, or Nachmanides, says, "Whatever has happened to the patriarchs is a sign to the children."[2] Our forefathers Abraham, Isaac and Jacob prophetically enacted in advance the history of their descendants, as did Jacob's sons, Joseph and his brothers. Joseph, then, is a sign to Israel that one whom we will reject and cast out of our midst will become our deliverer. Accordingly, rabbinic literature includes references to a Messiah ben Yosef, Messiah the son of Joseph, as early as this citation from the Talmud:

> What is the cause of the mourning [mentioned in Zechariah 12:12]?—Rabbi Dosa and the Rabbis differ on the point. R. Dosa explained, *The cause is the slaying of Messiah the son of Joseph* . . . since that well agrees with the Scriptural verse, *And they shall look upon me because they have thrust him through, and they shall mourn for him as one mourneth for his only son.* (Sukkah 52a)[3]

The Midrash and other rabbinic literature provide additional references to Messiah ben Joseph. [4] When Christian and Messianic Jewish readers think of Messiah son of Joseph, however, they're likely to remember the son "as was supposed" of a different Joseph, the son named Yeshua (Luke 3:23). This Yeshua ben Yosef, like Joseph in our story, is the favored son, who, like Joseph, experiences rejection by his own brothers, and is turned over to the Gentiles—not Egypt, as was Joseph, but its successor, Rome. He is accused of blasphemy, a capital offense in Jewish law,[5] and of challenging Roman rule, a capital crime under the empire.[6] In a collusion between the Jewish religious authorities and the Roman government, which alone had the power of capital punishment, Yeshua was sentenced to death by crucifixion.

In a striking parallel between this son of Joseph and the original Joseph, we see Yeshua also stripped of his clothing.

> They stripped off his clothes and put on him a scarlet robe, wove thorn-branches into a crown and put it on his head, and put a stick in his right hand. Then they kneeled down in front of him and made fun of him: "Hail to the King of the Jews!" They spit on him and used the stick to beat him about the head. (Matt. 27:28–30)

For a moment Yeshua's nakedness is covered with a special garment. The scarlet robe in this passage, like Joseph's *ketonet passim*, is a high-status garment. Richly colored dyes were costly in the ancient world, and this robe, although probably part of standard Roman military gear, suggested status.

> The "scarlet" robe (27:28) is undoubtedly a faded red soldier's cloak, which Mark (15:17) and John (19:2) apparently independently describe as "purple," reflecting the color of garments worn by hellenistic princes, hence the soldiers' mockery.[7]

The Roman soldiers intend mockery when they put this robe on Yeshua, along with a "crown" woven of thorn-branches, but despite their intention, they're displaying his real status. In John's account, Pilate brings Yeshua, wearing the crown of thorns and purple robe, before the crowd of his accusers and announces, "*Ecce homo*—Behold the man!" (John 19:5). Again, Pilate may have intended his words as mockery, but they highlight Yeshua's status as "the man," the one uniquely chosen to bring deliverance to Israel and all humankind. The Romans may have intended to mock Yeshua with the high-status purple robe, but in this case the garment of status and the garment of election have become one. The one wearing the purple robe is indeed the chosen one.

But Yeshua is again stripped, echoing the repeated times when Joseph was stripped of his garments, before attaining the true garment of chosen service.

> When they had finished ridiculing him, they took off the robe, put his own clothes back on him and led him away to be nailed to the execution-stake. . . . After they had nailed him to the stake, they divided his clothes among them by throwing dice. (Matt. 27:31, 35)

The Romans routinely crucified their victims naked, to increase the shame, humiliation and cruelty of this horrible form of execution.[8] When the soldiers cast lots for Yeshua's garments, they unknowingly fulfilled words penned by David centuries before: "They divide my garments among themselves; for my clothing they throw dice" (Ps. 22:19 [v. 18 in Christian Bibles]).[9] Yeshua is not only stripped and exposed to public shame, but is completely deprived of his garments altogether, as his torturers divide them among themselves.

The great mystery of God's favor is that now in his humiliation, Messiah is clothed in the true garment of election, at which the robe of royal purple can only hint. In the shame of crucifixion, Messiah Yeshua's glory is revealed.

> Yeshua gave them this answer: "The time has come for the Son of Man to be glorified. Yes, indeed! I tell you that unless a grain of wheat that falls to the ground dies, it stays just a grain; but if it dies, it produces a big harvest. . . .

> "Now I am in turmoil. What can I say—'Father, save me from this hour'? No, it was for this very reason that I have come to this hour. . . . As for me, when I am lifted up from the earth, I will draw everyone to myself." He said this to indicate what kind of death he would die. (John 12:23–24, 27, 32–33)

> And when the centurion, who stood facing him, saw that in this way he breathed his last, he said, "Truly this man was the Son of God!" (Mark 15:39, ESV)

Messiah's glory and sonship are revealed, not through kingly garments, but through the humblest garb—the shameful garb—that he must wear to accomplish the Father's purposes.

Messiah's sufferings are unique, of course, but they reveal a mysterious dimension of favor that will lead us beyond rivalry and discord to a new and better way. God allows the garment of favor to be stripped away so a deeper meaning of favor can eventually be revealed. In the same way, the removal of Joseph's garment of status launched a long and tortuous journey that finally revealed the true meaning of his election. And so it is with all those who claim to know and represent the God of Israel—being favored in this way isn't meant to be a source of status, power or religious privilege. Instead, it's an election to service that benefits all, and if need be, even to suffering. Its garment isn't the noble tunic, but the coveralls of service.

## The Garment of Hypocrisy

One reason I've undertaken this study of Joseph is that the notion of favor, which has so much potential to expand and enrich our lives today, creates a lot of pushback. The idea of a favored child or a favored people stirs up great resistance in our day of inclusion and equal opportunity. It's an idea that's not going to gain a record number of likes on Facebook. Of course arbitrary exclusiveness is a bad thing, and equal opportunity for success and happiness is a worthy goal. But the God of Israel, the God described in Scripture, reserves the right to favor and choose individuals, communities and nations for his own reasons. The story of Joseph's clothing and unclothing, beginning with his ornamented tunic and finally ending with the garments of an Egyptian noble, reveals this favor isn't about status and prestige. It's about entering your assigned place in God's master plan, and serving others there. When the ultimate favored one appears, he embodies this same truth, and allows himself to be stripped of all status to serve humankind.

Can this understanding of favor be relevant in today's increasingly secular world? I believe it can, if those who claim a connection to God will set aside the bogus tunic of status and put on the authentic garment of favor, the coveralls of service.

Wearing a bogus garment reminds me of Yeshua's use of the term "hypocrite" to critique some of the religious folk of his day:

> "So, when you do *tzedakah*, don't announce it with trumpets to win people's praise, like the hypocrites in the synagogues and on the streets. Yes! I tell you, they have their reward already!"

"When you pray, don't be like the hypocrites, who love to pray standing in the synagogues and on street corners, so that people can see them. Yes! I tell you, they have their reward already!"

"Now when you fast, don't go around looking miserable, like the hypocrites. They make sour faces so that people will know they are fasting. Yes! I tell you, they have their reward already!" (Matt. 6:2, 5, 16)

Yeshua called out the hypocrites, and hypocrisy may be the most common charge raised against religious folk today, whether Christian or Jewish. You can judge for yourself whether it's a fair critique, but it is relevant to our discussion of favor. Favor is a stumbling-block when the favored one wears it as a status symbol, and Yeshua calls this sort of behavior hypocrisy. The hypocrite is one who uses legitimate religious practices, like giving, prayer, and fasting, as status-markers, "so that people can see them." When Messiah says "they have their reward already," he's referring to the reward of status and recognition, which the hypocrites pursue instead of seeking to fulfill God's purpose.

A few years back, David Kinnaman wrote a book analyzing the declining influence and increasingly negative image of Christianity among young people. One outsider interviewed in the book put it this way: "Most people I meet assume that Christian means very conservative, entrenched in their thinking, antigay, antichoice, angry, violent, illogical, empire builders; they want to convert everyone, and they generally cannot live peacefully with anyone who doesn't believe what they believe." Kinnaman comments,

What are Christians known for? Outsiders think our moralizing, our condemnations, and our attempts to draw boundaries around everything. Even if these standards are accurate and biblical, they seem to be all we have to offer. And our lives are a poor advertisement for the standards. We have set the gameboard to register lifestyle points; then we are surprised to be trapped by our mistakes. The truth is we have invited the hypocrite image.[10]

Judaism, according to current polls, at least in America, has a much better public image than Christianity, especially Evangelical Christianity of the sort that Kinnaman describes. Still, Jews who grew up in the synagogue and left often cite hypocrisy as their big turn-off. Here are a couple of examples I pulled almost randomly from the Internet. They don't use the word "hypocrisy," but describe it well enough. In one example, "Why I Left the Synagogue," writer Judy Walters says she and her husband wanted to be active in their congregation, but became frustrated after serving on various ineffective committees:

> So, we joined a program called *Chavurah*, where young couples and families came together to form close circles, like extended families, for both Jewish and secular events. We started off really liking it; we felt like we had a home and a nice group of friends at last. But soon, it began to feel like a chore. Members fought over who would bring what to events. Members sided with each other in petty disagreements, and gossip was rampant. We were one of only two couples without young children. We felt left out of things. We left the *Chavurah*.[11]

Another blogger, who writes under the moniker "The Jewish Atheist," recounts:

> When I was a child, I remembered High Holiday services at our hometown temple as glorified fashion shows and gossip fests. The rabbi and cantor were speaking or singing while

the congregants whispered about who looked old, who got divorced, or where so-and-so's daughter went to college. The most religious time of the Jewish year was reduced to petty arguments, icy glares, and idle chatter. The sanctuary was filled with warm bodies, but mentally, many of the congregants were elsewhere.[12]

In all these examples, Jewish and Christian, the "garments" of religious tradition and practice obscure the real message. Joseph, and Messiah ben Joseph after him, shed their outward garments to reveal the mantle of sacrificial service, which is the authentic outfit of favor. The garment, the status marker, is inherently deceptive, even as its name in Hebrew suggests: *Beged* (garment) is from the same root as *bagad* (deceive or betray). It's no accident *beged*/garment appears twice in the account of Tamar's deception of Judah, and five times in the story of Potiphar's wife framing Joseph. Garments, as part of outward appearances, are inherently deceptive. Left to ourselves, we seek to clothe our nakedness, not with what God has truly made us to be, but with some pretense, some persona of our own making, only to meet with inevitable reversal. This reversal, however, often turns out to be redemptive, and if we follow the example of Messiah we willingly relinquish the garments of status to put on the coveralls of service.

Family is meant to be the place where people can see us without our fancy garments, where whatever we might have been trying to disguise or downplay with our wardrobe is on display. The young Joseph in his garment of favor might look impressive to an outsider, but to his brothers, the garment only sets off his annoying and unworthy qualities. As the story goes, a guy made a lot of money on the stock market and bought himself a big yacht and dressed up as a captain. When his mother asks him why he's wearing such a snappy uniform, he says, "Mama, look at my yacht—I'm a captain now." She replies, "Well, by you you're a captain, and maybe by me you're a captain, but by a captain you're no captain!" The captain's uniform doesn't make you a captain—and our family members often remind us of that. Family is the place where we are delivered from our pretenses and can be, or become, who we are meant to be—at least ideally. That's why the process of differentiation discussed earlier insists we remain connected to family, even as we become our own men and women.

## The Dream-Master

For Joseph, remaining connected to his family is a huge challenge, and the way he accomplishes it, after he finally acquires the garments of true favor and service in the court of Egypt, might help us in our efforts to remain connected. We'll discuss this process in detail when it reaches its conclusion in our next *parasha*. But first, let's turn our attention to another theme that runs through multiple chapters—dreams.

Earlier in our story (Gen. 37:19), when Joseph's brothers saw him approaching from a distance, they said *Hineh ba'al ha-chalomot*, literally, "Look, the dream-master!" In the original Hebrew, this phrase wasn't quite as sarcastic as it sounds in English, because the noun *ba'al* was frequently used in conjunction with another noun (in this case, "dreams") to simply mean an owner or possessor of that thing. In his brothers' eyes, Joseph was the owner of two outrageous dreams, in which he saw himself dominating not only them but his mother and father as well. The real problem, though, wasn't that Joseph had such dreams; he can hardly be faulted for images that come to him when he's asleep. Rather, he's at fault for being so eager to tell his family about the dreams, and gloating over their implied message. And so, after Joseph recounted his first dream, in which sheaves gathered by his brothers bowed down to the sheaf he had gathered, his brothers "hated him still more for his dreams and for what he said." After the second, in which the sun, moon, and eleven stars bowed down to him, "his father rebuked him: 'What is this dream you have had? Do you really expect me, your mother and your brothers to come and prostrate ourselves before you on the ground?'" (Gen. 37:5–10).

It's no wonder Joseph's brothers focus on him as the dream-master when they're psyching themselves up to get rid of him. Joseph's act of telling these dreams to his brothers had ramped up the sibling rivalry and revealed how little he understood of his real role as the favored son. Like his noble tunic, Joseph wore his dreams as a sign of status and prestige.

From a family-dynamics perspective, there's another problem with these dreams—or at least with the dreamer, and the way he handles the dreams. The two dreams reveal his mission, the life-assignment God will ensure he fulfills. Okay, but why does he need to *announce* that mission to everyone around him? It looks like Joseph has gained an inflated sense of his mission before he has gained a more foundational sense of his worth in God's sight. He announces his mission to let it be known how worthy he is—perhaps because he's not so sure he really is all that worthy. His father, older and wiser, demonstrates what should have been Joseph's approach: "His father kept the matter in mind."

Joseph's recounting of his dreams illustrates a concept I'll call by the fancy phrase "instrumental election." This is the idea that God chooses someone, or some specific group or nation, primarily to be an instrument of his will, primarily as a means to accomplish some divine end. This idea often comes up in discussions of God's election of Israel as his chosen people. For example, New Testament scholar NT Wright says, "The God of Israel had called Israel into being in order to save the world; that was the purpose of election in the first place." Wright is a brilliant and original scholar, but here he lines up with much faulty Christian thinking throughout the ages. "Israel, the chosen people, has failed to accomplish the mission to which she was called. That is, Israel as a whole has failed; Israel's representative, the Messiah, Jesus, has succeeded."[13] In this view, Israel is chosen primarily, or even solely, for a purpose, and if it fails in this purpose, it gets unchosen. Or, to put it more accurately, Israel's national, ethnic election gets reformatted in the church, which is the new elect, the fulfillment of God's purposes for Israel. As the great nineteenth-century preacher CH Spurgeon put it in his commentary on the Book of Psalms,

> The Lord loves the gates of Zion more than all. It is here assumed that the Lord loves the dwellings of Jacob. He loves those that are true Israelites. These are succeeded by the name Christian, for the Christian Church is now become the true Israel of God.[14]

Examples of this sort of replacement theology abound. My point is simply that if we emphasize instrumental election—seeing God's choice of a person or group, or of ourselves, as primarily functional, that is, primarily to accomplish a mission—and the chosen one doesn't fulfill that mission, then the election itself is called into question.

In this view, God chose Israel to be an instrument of blessing for all nations, specifically through bringing forth the Messiah. Therefore, God can dispense with Israel once Israel has accomplished its task—a dangerous idea, as history has proven. An instrumental view is also dangerous because it feeds religious extremism and abuse. If I've been chosen for a mission, I'd better accomplish it no matter who or what stands in my way, or else I might get unchosen. But the radical truth of Scripture is that God does not treat humans as a means to an end. He chooses Israel because of his love (Dt. 4:37, 7:6–11). The favored one must learn to rest in God's favor, which is motivated solely by God's love for him, before trying to accomplish any purpose for which he was chosen.

Let's consider one ramification of the instrumental emphasis that plays out in Joseph's family. Joseph seems to get a sense of his *purpose* as a chosen one before he's fully grounded in his God-given *worth* as the chosen one. He thinks he is chosen, to use Wright's phrase, "in order to save the world," or at least his own family, when in fact he is chosen first simply out of his father's love—love that Joseph might not deserve or even *need to deserve* in order to be chosen. This is the meaning of "favor"—it is ultimately not rational or consistent, but motivated by love and desire. Because he's favored, Joseph will become the means of accomplishing the big mission for his family. But it's favor first, mission second. This might seem a subtle distinction, but it's essential to understanding favor properly. First, as we've seen above, if mission has priority and you fail in your mission, you're liable to get unchosen—which is what Christian theology has often said happens to Israel. Second, if mission has priority, you're driven to flaunt and accomplish your mission to *prove* you're chosen. This seems to be Joseph's motivation to flaunt his dreams and make sure his brothers understood their message about him. I suspect he was also motivated by a need to reassure himself. This misunderstanding of favor is dangerous, and is a major factor behind the religious zeal and self-exaltation that is one of the evils of our times.

Rabbi Jonathan Sacks opens his remarkable study of religious violence with a quote by the great French thinker Blaise Pascal: "Men never do evil so completely and cheerfully as when they do it from religious conviction," He goes on to quote a survivor of a massacre by the Nigerian Islamist group Boko Haram: "They told us they were doing God's work even though all the men they shot in front of me were Muslims. They seemed happy." [15] Were they happy because they had a chance to prove their devotion to the cause, their worthiness to be among the chosen? I believe a motivating factor in religious evil—a motive that can turn seemingly ordinary people into murderers—is a twisted sense of favor. Someone believes he is chosen for a purpose, but has no security, no real identity in being so favored, so he has to fulfill that purpose to prove he deserves it.

Joseph, of course, doesn't come anywhere close to all this. My point is that his youthful dreams of dominance, and his folly in telling his family of them, reflect the idea of instrumental election: "I'm chosen for a purpose, and I have to make sure that purpose gets accomplished, no matter what." From this perspective, anyone who opposes that purpose, or even just fails to recognize it (like Joseph's brothers at first) doesn't deserve much consideration. This is the essence of zero-sum favor. It's a dangerous idea, with the potential to fuel dogmatic violence, as we can see in recent world events. Instead, what must come first is the security and confidence that arise from knowing you're favored out of the kindness of the parental figure, the confidence instilled by a positive, loving family environment. Ultimately we're talking about boundless favor; you don't deserve it, and don't have to, but you use your position of favor to serve others. We can only hope to see this idea overcome the epidemic of religious violence in our world someday, but right now it can have a powerful impact on our own lives and within our families and communities.

## A leader emerges

Joseph's story involves three pairs of dreams, and it's only the first pair that he doesn't interpret, possibly because the meaning is so obvious that the dreams need no interpretation. In this first pair, Joseph is the hero, and the entire story of Joseph and his brothers is a fulfillment of this first pair of dreams. Now, as the climax of Joseph's story approaches here in *Parashat Mikketz*, his brothers will appear before him after he has been promoted by Pharaoh, and bow low to him with their faces to the ground. Joseph will recognize his brothers, but they won't recognize him, and Joseph will remember the first pair dreams, which he had dreamed about them (Gen. 42:6–9). The dreams were true, and God's choice of him was true, and it will finally come full circle after twenty-two difficult years.

This scene comes near the beginning of a lengthy and complicated test Joseph imposes on his brothers, from his position of power and service in Egypt. Joseph is in charge of administering the food supply, which he had wisely created after interpreting Pharaoh's dreams as a warning of impending famine. The famine spreads to all the surrounding peoples, and Jacob sends ten of his sons down to Egypt to buy food, but keeps his new favorite, Benjamin, with him at home.

We might wonder why all ten brothers need to go down to Egypt. Couldn't two or three have been sent with a few servants to accomplish the task? But we shouldn't be surprised, because throughout the story, the brothers generally act as a group—in resenting Joseph, plotting against him, selling him into slavery, deceiving their father, and now in going down to Egypt to obtain food from the unrecognized Joseph. This behavior reflects the power of family to create a sense of belonging or, negatively, of groupthink, the pressure of the crowd, the herd instinct. Family is an institution in which one can lose one's identity. In the Introduction, we saw that identity formation entails "both a sense of belonging and a sense of being separate."[16] In the ancient world, the sense of belonging, of being part of something larger than oneself, especially family, was clearly dominant. Indeed, I believe we often misinterpret biblical stories by reading them through the lenses of individualism. But even in the ancient world of the Bible, individual identity, "a sense of being separate," played an essential part in shaping a human life. Before Joseph's test of his brothers ends, it will require that one of the brothers separate himself and step forth from the group, to meet the challenge on behalf of all the others. In the meantime, it's not so surprising they all go down to Egypt together, but it highlights that Benjamin doesn't go. He's the new favorite, the object of favoritism just as Joseph had been long before. The ten sons can take the dangerous trip to Egypt, but apparently Jacob isn't willing to risk his son Benjamin.

When the ten brothers arrive, Joseph accuses them of coming to Egypt to spy out the land, not to buy food. They try to defend themselves and mention their elderly father, and their youngest brother, Benjamin, in the process. Joseph demands they return to Egypt with their little brother, and he holds Simeon hostage until they return. At this point in the story, our attention shifts from Joseph to two other brothers, Reuben and Judah. We're back to our sub-theme of differentiation, "the capacity to be an 'I' while remaining connected," as Rabbi Friedman puts it. The differentiated individual remains part of the family, but no longer just goes along with the family. Instead, he's being prepared to act dramatically, even sacrificially, on behalf of the family. Joseph had to be separated from his family to become differentiated; he became his own person, but he didn't abandon his family. In fact, his testing of his brothers is designed to enable him to reconnect with his family, and provide for their safety and restoration.

But for now, the focus is on Reuben, the biological firstborn, and Judah, who is next in line, because Simeon and Levi, who follow after Reuben in birth order, eliminated themselves from consideration by their outrageous attack on Shechem (ch. 34). Reuben weakened his claim by sleeping with his father's concubine (35:22), but he seems to be trying to get back in the running. Along with Judah he will seek to differentiate himself as a leader in response to Joseph's test.

Let's consider Reuben first. Years before, when he heard his brothers plotting against Joseph, he tried to save him by persuading them to throw Joseph into a pit instead of killing him. He planned to rescue Joseph and restore him to his father, but while Reuben was absent or not paying attention, Joseph was drawn out of the pit and sold into slavery. When Reuben returned and heard what happened to Joseph, he rejoined his brothers in their scheme to cover up the crime and deceive their father (37:21ff.). Reuben's attempt at differentiation failed. Now, the brothers need to bring Benjamin with them on their return trip to Egypt to ransom Simeon and buy more food. Jacob refuses to send him, and Reuben tries to stand out from the pack again by convincing his father to send Benjamin. He tells him, "If I don't bring him back to you, you can kill my own two sons! Put him in my care; I will return him to you." Jacob, of course, refuses, "My son will not go down with you" (42:37–38). The Midrash imagines Jacob thinking of Reuben, "He is indeed a foolish firstborn! Are not your sons my sons!" Indeed, the Midrash adds that centuries later, if someone spoke nonsense in the presence of Rabbi Tarfon (second century CE), he would remark, "My son shall not go down with you!", citing the example of the foolish Reuben (*Genesis Rabbah* 91:9). He fails again to differentiate himself.

Judah's attempt at differentiation is more successful, and will provide the turning point for the whole family drama. As we saw in *Parashat Vayeshev*, Judah had modeled repentance in the incident with Tamar. He was able to see and even admit publicly that his daughter-in-law was in the right and he himself was in the wrong. Repentance is a form of differentiation because it requires one to become an "I" who isn't just swept along by events, but takes responsibility for doing the right thing. Repentance also reflects differentiation because it requires the one who is repentant to stay connected. He has to go back to family members and others he's harmed or offended and make amends. He can't complete his repentance if he doesn't stay connected.

Judah has done all this, and so he's already a well-differentiated man when it comes time to return to Egypt with Benjamin. To persuade Jacob to send Benjamin, in contrast with the overblown offer of Reuben, who is still trying to differentiate himself, Judah simply says,

> "Send the boy with me; and we will make preparations and leave; so that we may stay alive and not die, both we and you, and also our little ones. I myself will guarantee his safety; you can hold me responsible. If I fail to bring him to you and present him to your face, let me bear the blame forever." (43:8–9)

Judah's calm and realistic offer is compelling to Jacob, and he releases Benjamin into his care. Judah, Benjamin and all the brothers go down to Egypt (except for Simeon, who is still there as Joseph's hostage), obtain the food they need for their family's survival, and start home with Simeon as well. But before

*Parashat Mikketz* reaches its conclusion, Joseph has Benjamin framed and arrested for stealing a silver goblet. The brothers all return in anguish to Joseph's court with Benjamin the accused. True to his word, Judah steps forward from the rest to begin his plea for Benjamin's release:

> "There's nothing we can say to my lord! How can we speak? There's no way we can clear ourselves! God has revealed your servants' guilt; so here we are, my lord's slaves—both we and also the one in whose possession the cup was found." (44:16)

Judah's words "God has revealed your servants' guilt" are rich with irony. In part, he's referring to their "guilt" for stealing the goblet, which didn't actually happen. But he's also thinking of the guilt they truly *do* bear for selling Joseph, a crime—and guilt—in which all the brothers except Benjamin had a share. The Midrash paraphrases Judah's statement: "The Creditor has now found the opportunity of exacting his debt" (*Genesis Rabbah* 92:9). In other words, Judah is thinking, "At last, God will make us pay for what we did to Joseph." Perhaps it's for this reason, because all the brothers have a share in the guilt of selling Joseph, that Judah proposes all the brothers remain as slaves in Egypt. But of course this is a crazy offer, which may reflect the panicked state of Judah's thinking as he faces "a dilemma that involves agonizing decisions."

> They can save their own lives, but this would be disastrous to their father and would be at the expense of their loyalty to Benjamin. If the brothers stay with Benjamin, they cannot bring back food to their father and to their families, who will then die of starvation.[17]

Joseph simplifies matters for Judah and returns the focus to the real issue behind his manipulative testing. He rejects Judah's crazy offer: "Heaven forbid that I should act in such a way. The man in whose possession the goblet was found will be my slave; but as for you, go in peace to your father" (43:17). Literally Joseph says, "And you (plural) go up in *shalom*—peace, wholeness, wellbeing—to your father." Again, the words are rich with irony. How can the brothers go back "in shalom" without Benjamin? Yet Joseph is highlighting something essential to the dynamics of family, because families often do opt for a false peace that sacrifices one member—the scapegoat—to stabilize things for the rest of the members. This is exactly what the brothers did, or attempted to do, by selling out Joseph years earlier. Now Joseph is setting up Benjamin to be a new scapegoat, to bear all the brothers' resentments of their father's favoritism on his shoulders. What's at stake here, however, isn't the false peace a scapegoat can create, but *true* peace for this family, which has suffered the opposite of peace for at least the past 22 years. This is what's at stake as our *parasha* concludes, and the spotlight is on Judah, who has spoken up to plead for his family. How will he respond to this offer of a shallow peace?

# Chapter Three

# *Vayigash*
# "And he drew near"

*Then Yehudah drew near to him . . .*

*Parashat Vayigash* brings us to the climax of the whole story of Joseph and his brothers. You could even say we reach the climax with the very first Hebrew word of the parasha, *Vayigash*—"He drew near"—as Judah approaches Joseph with a heart-wrenching appeal: "O my lord, please let your servant speak a word in my lord's ears, and do not let your anger burn against your servant; for you are as Pharaoh" (Gen. 44:18, author's translation). He pleads for mercy upon his aged father, the one who will suffer most if Benjamin is imprisoned. Judah repeats the word "father" fourteen times in his appeal before he ends with this astounding offer: "Therefore, please let your servant remain as a slave to my lord instead of the boy, and let the boy go back with his brothers" (Gen. 44:33, JPS TANAKH).

Joseph is so moved by Judah's offer that he can't maintain his disguise, or his distance, any longer; he orders all his attendants to leave the room, and reveals himself to his brothers: "*Ani Yosef. Ha'od avi chai*—I am Joseph! Is my father still alive?" (45:3).

Yes, this is the turning point of the whole story, but why? At its core, this is the story of the restoration of Jacob's family, the household of Israel. Long before the family was threatened by famine, it had been torn apart by Jacob's open favoritism toward Joseph, Joseph's flaunting of his favor, and the brothers' bitter resentment and revenge. The family is broken. Betrayal and distrust permeate the entire system. Now, Joseph's orchestration of events has created the opportunity for restored trust and brotherhood, and Judah steps up—or draws near—to respond to that opportunity.

The famed attorney Alan Dershowitz, in his book *The Genesis of Justice*, portrays Joseph's testing of his brothers as "a grand retributive scheme," a "retaliatory prank" that teaches them "a lesson about how it feels to be victimized by those more powerful than you." Based on this reading, Dershowitz claims "Joseph was, of course, going to do the right thing regardless of the nature of [Judah's] plea"—the "right thing" being to release Benjamin and let the brothers off the hook.[1] And if Joseph's goal is simply to teach his brothers a lesson, that's probably true. But Joseph is actually after something greater than this, the healing of the entire family of Jacob. The main character in the whole drama is neither Joseph nor Judah, but the father, Jacob. Only as the sons of Jacob come to embrace and support their father's choice can the family be restored.

Remember, one of Joseph's most pronounced character traits is his commitment to the interests of his superior. This is the trait that explains, on the human level, his repeated ascent to positions of responsibility and power. He is all in for what matters to his superior—especially his father. We saw this trait in the first few verses of his story: "When Yosef was seventeen years old he used to pasture the flock with his brothers, even though he was still a boy. Once when he was with the sons of Bilhah and the sons of Zilpah, his father's wives, he brought a bad report about them to their father. Now Isra'el loved Yosef the most of all his children"

(37:2–3a). Joseph may have been oblivious to what his brothers thought of him, but he was totally focused on his father's interests. Accordingly, the brothers resented Joseph, but Jacob rewarded his loyalty with more responsibility. In Egypt, Joseph displayed the same fierce loyalty to Potiphar, to the master of the dungeon, and finally to Pharaoh himself. But even as the second-in-command over all Egypt, Joseph remains loyal above all to his father. So his testing of his brothers is not "a retaliatory prank," but a carefully designed opportunity for them to prove their own loyalty to the father. In other words, Joseph tests his brothers to see whether he can finally trust them to do right by their father. He can't reveal himself to them, and the family can't begin to be restored, until he determines whether they can be trusted.

## Steps in restoring trust

Joseph's test of his brothers reveals much about the dynamics of trust, an essential element in building and sustaining family, whether a nuclear, extended or community one. We need trust. Trust in each other, in our leaders, and ultimately in God. But we can't just demand it. When someone we don't know well says, "Just trust me," our response is likely to be, "Yeah, right!" We trust that person *less*, not more, because they haven't earned our trust. Though trust must be earned, you have to give the other person the *chance* to earn it. Trust must be extended by the one who has been offended or betrayed. Only then can the offender begin the task of regaining the trust he has destroyed.

Let's retrace the story of Joseph's test of his brothers to see the stages in restoring trust, which have bearing on how we restore or deepen trust in our own families and communities. We can trace three steps the brothers take to *earn* trust, framed by two ways in which Joseph *extends* trust enough to give the brothers a chance to earn it.

## Joseph *extends* trust by identifying the heart of the issue.

Joseph zeroes in on the brothers' attitude toward Benjamin, the (new) favored son, which ultimately reflects their attitude toward the father. He mercifully extends enough trust to let them prove themselves in that essential and very sensitive issue. Ironically, Joseph launches this trust-building process by accusing his brothers of coming to Egypt as spies. He could have simply gotten his sweet revenge on them as soon as they showed up in his court, by throwing them all in prison, or worse. Or he could have just dropped the whole thing, let bygones be bygones, and brought the family back together without all the drama that takes up two chapters of Genesis. But he still wouldn't have been able to trust his brothers, and the family still wouldn't be healed of their betrayal and rejection.

Often, when there's a breakdown in trust, the offended party is tempted to cut off communication with the offender entirely, or if that's not possible, to pretend like everything is just fine and conceal the sense of betrayal and distrust. The offended party retreats into a stronghold of bitterness and resentment, punishing the offender with silence and loss of intimacy. It won't do to urge the offended party to just forgive and forget—they are already pretending to do that. For trust to be restored, then as now, the one who's been betrayed needs to identify the essential issue. He or she needs to identify what the offender did to lose trust, and what the offender can do to begin to rebuild it. It's not a black-and-white, either total-trust or zero-trust sort of thing. Trust is restored incrementally. The one who's been betrayed can't just magically start trusting again, but he or she can identify how the trust was lost and what the offender can do to start regaining it, step by step.

For Joseph, the issue is whether the brothers who betrayed him twenty years earlier will now act like brothers—especially toward the favored brother, Benjamin. So Joseph pursued an elaborate process that began when he first grilled his brothers and accused them of being spies. When they denied it, he said,

> By this you shall be *put to the test*: unless your youngest brother comes here, by Pharaoh, you shall not depart from this place! Let one of you go and bring your brother, while the rest of you remain confined, that your words may be *put to the test* whether there is truth in you. (Gen. 42:15–16 JPS TANAKH, emphasis added)

The brothers probably assumed the test was meant to determine whether they even *had* a younger brother, as they had told Joseph, which would prove they really were ten sons of one father, and not ten spies. But the *real* test was to see how they would treat the new favorite son, Benjamin, after their abusive mistreatment of the old favorite son, Joseph. Note the irony here: Joseph says he's testing whether they're spies, but he's really testing whether they care about their brother, and even more, whether they will finally respect Jacob their father and his choice of a favorite. He's extending enough trust to let them prove themselves in the specific way that matters. Extending trust in this way is an act of faith with the power to create more trust—if the brothers respond.

► **Step one in *earning* trust: The brothers show authentic, articulated remorse.**

Joseph's test triggers the brothers' first step in earning his trust.

> They said to each other, "We are in fact guilty concerning our brother. He was in distress and pleaded with us; we saw it and wouldn't listen. That's why this distress has

come upon us now." Re'uven answered them, "Didn't I tell you, 'Don't wrong the boy'? But you wouldn't hear of it. Now comes the reckoning for his blood!" They had no idea that Yosef understood them, since an interpreter was translating for them. *Yosef turned away from them and wept.* (42:21–24, emphasis added)

The brothers' remorse isn't the usual "I'm sorry if you were offended" sort of thing we hear so often today. Instead, the brothers express three characteristics of true remorse, which will provide a basis for their restoration. First, they recognize the specifics of their wrongdoing—what exactly they did wrong—and they put it into words. This is what is called "confession" in many religious traditions. Second, they understand the emotional impact of their wrongdoing on the one they wronged. In contrast with the "I'm sorry if you were offended" variety of confession, they understand and admit how offensive their actions were. It's not your being offended that's the problem, but my offensive behavior. Third, they see the connection between their wrongdoing and their current circumstances. They got themselves into this mess.

I often deal with trust in counseling married couples, for example one couple I'll call Tom and Brenda. Tom was a hardworking, middle-aged guy and Brenda had caught him in an affair. He broke it off immediately, told Brenda he was really sorry, promised he would never do it again, and started acting like the ideal husband. Brenda didn't trust him, of course, and asked lots of questions about the other woman, how they met, when they last saw each other, and so on—often at really inappropriate times. She also found it hard to be affectionate with Tom. He grew frustrated and told Brenda, "I admitted what I did and said I'm sorry; what more do you want from me?"

When they came for counseling, I had to remind Tom he had gotten himself into this doghouse, and needed to be patient with Brenda's distance and distrust. He needed to answer her questions as a sign of his remorse. As he took responsibility for causing the marital breakdown, and stopped trying to get Brenda to respond differently, recovery could begin.

Likewise, Joseph can't act on his brothers' remorse alone, but it is their first step in earning his trust. When he hears their words, Joseph turns away and weeps, not because everything is now fixed, but because he gets a glimpse into his brothers' hearts, and sees their hearts are broken over what they've done— a critical moment in the trust-restoring process. In our own process, we sometimes make Tom's mistake of thinking remorse alone should earn trust—or that others should trust us simply because we've shown remorse. Or, if we're the one who's been offended, we make the opposite mistake of ignoring the heart change that underlies genuine remorse, and remaining unmoved. When it's genuine, we can affirm remorse, though it is only a step, and has to be followed by action.

▶ **Step two: Judah takes clear, concrete, and credible responsibility.**

Instead of jailing all the brothers and letting one return home, as he threatened, Joseph confines just one, Simeon, and lets all the rest return home. It's another test: Will they come back with Benjamin to rescue Simeon, or let Simeon end up a slave, just as they let Joseph end up a slave? As it turns out, when the brothers arrive home, they do want to go back to Egypt with Benjamin, but Jacob is hesitant—until Judah steps forward to take responsibility for Benjamin's return. He makes a real commitment, not a blasé "don't worry about it," nor a wild, overblown proposal like Reuben's offer to let Jacob kill his two sons if he returns without Benjamin. Judah, in contrast with Reuben, earns Jacob's trust (and the chance to earn Joseph's) with a clear, concrete, credible commitment: "I myself will be surety for him; you may hold me responsible: if I do not bring him back to you and set him before you, I shall stand guilty before you forever" (Gen. 43:9, JPS TANAKH). Jacob doesn't realize it, and Judah himself might not realize it, but he is taking the responsibility he'd shunned twenty-plus years earlier, when he failed to bring his younger brother home to the father. Now he's taking responsibility not just for what he did, but for the consequences as well. Whether he's conscious of all this or not, Jacob entrusts him with Benjamin.

Taking responsibility by making a specific, believable commitment remains a potent step in replenishing the reserve of trust. Sadly, in our day, people tend to shy away from commitment. Men in particular seem averse to making any kind of commitment at all, or they make superficial commitments to create a temporary good feeling, but don't follow through. That maneuver is deadly when trust has been lost. Tom was willing to tell Brenda that his affair was all his fault, and that he'd never do it again, but he had to make more immediate and specific commitments. For example, he could commit to hearing Brenda out whenever she had doubts or questions, answering everything as thoroughly as he could, and not expecting her to just get over it. As he followed through on that specific, measurable commitment, Brenda might start to trust him more. His bigger commitment to "never do it again" might become more believable. To earn trust, we need to take responsibility for what we've done to lose that trust, and for what we'll do to regain it. We need to make clear commitments, even seemingly minor ones, and follow through without fail. Judah is about to provide another example of what that means.

When Judah and the rest of the brothers arrive with Benjamin, Joseph arranges things to remind them Benjamin is the new favorite, and to flush out any resentment still lingering among the brothers. By demanding they bring Benjamin on their next journey, he had already put the spotlight on Jacob's favoritism. After all, why was Jacob willing to risk all his other sons by sending them down to Egypt, but not this one? Why was he willing to let Simeon sit in jail, and risk starvation for the rest of his family, just to protect Benjamin? Finally, when Jacob lets Benjamin go to Egypt with his brothers and they arrive together, Joseph invites all the brothers to eat with him, then seats them in order of birth. He gives Benjamin, the youngest, the portion of honor—five times that of his brothers' (Gen. 43:34). Benjamin isn't wearing a *ketonet passim* as Joseph had, but he's clearly marked as the favorite, and he's made a clear target for his brothers' envy. But then, in a stunning reversal, within a few hours the favored one is framed as a thief and ends up being arrested by Joseph, who offers to let everyone else go home in peace. How will the brothers act this time, when the son who is so obviously favored is once again in their power?

Alan Dershowitz says Joseph would have let everyone off the hook regardless of their response to his test, but I'm not so sure. Joseph already has Benjamin, his only full brother, the only other son of the favored wife Rachel, in his custody. Can we imagine him reconciling with the brothers had they decided not to rescue Benjamin, and instead tried to return to Jacob with supplies but without the chosen one? Joseph probably would have told them that they were unworthy of Benjamin, as they had been unworthy of him, and of the father that favored him.[2] If Joseph were inclined to be merciful, he might let his brothers return to Canaan with their food supply, but I imagine him going ahead of them in a swift chariot, along with Benjamin, to reveal himself to his father and escort him back to the safety of Egypt, leaving the brothers to fend for themselves.

► **Step three: Judah pays the price.**

Judah's actions, however, allow Plan A to unfold. He has made the commitment to bring Benjamin back to his father, and now he follows through, even at the cost of his own freedom. He offers himself in exchange for Benjamin.

> "For your servant himself guaranteed his safety; I said, 'If I fail to bring him to you, then I will bear the blame before my father forever.' Therefore, I beg you, let your servant stay as a slave to my lord instead of the boy, and let the boy go up with his brothers. For how can I go up to my father if the boy isn't with me? I couldn't bear to see my father so overwhelmed by anguish." (44:32–34)

The greatest trust-building measure is the one that costs. You can't just say you're sorry, even if you say it with deep and authentic remorse, and you can't just commit to change, even if it's a clear and measurable commitment. You have to pay whatever price the commitment demands. But remember, it's not just any act of self-denial that will gain trust, but self-denial for the right purpose. Tom had to pay the price of really listening to his wife, of cheerfully giving her the time and space to process her feelings about Tom and the affair. She might seem unreasonable and accusatory at times, but Tom pays the price by staying in the line of fire to help her work through her feelings, including those against him.

The trust-testing question that Joseph raises is this: They rejected Joseph when he was the favored one; will they now pay the price for Benjamin, the one their father favors in his place? Judah earns trust because he puts the father's desire and priority ahead of his own, regardless of the cost to himself. Only now does Joseph know he can trust his brothers to put the well-being of the family, and the honor of their father, ahead of themselves.

## Repentance and restoration of trust

Judah's offer of himself and his freedom in exchange for Benjamin, of his life for Benjamin's, is an act of repentance. The great Jewish sage Rambam, or Maimonides, described repentance centuries ago:

> What is complete repentance? When a person has the opportunity to commit the original sin again, and is physically able to sin again, but one doesn't sin because of his repentance. Not out of fear, or because of physical weakness. For example, if a man had forbidden sexual relations with a woman, and then at a later time found himself alone with her, even though he still loves her as much as before, and he has the physical strength to sin, and was in the same country as when he sinned, yet he refrains and does not sin, he is a *baal teshuva* ('master of repentance').[3]

In this passage, Rambam uses the Hebrew term *teshuva*, which means "turning" or "return." It's a better term than "repentance" because it's more concrete, and harder to dismiss as just a religious notion. *Teshuva* implies reaching a turning point, turning away from denial, blaming others, and making excuses. It means returning to take full responsibility for the mess we've made of our lives and what we need to do to clean it up.

Joseph's brothers had to practice *teshuva* over their rejection of Joseph or, better, over their decision to put themselves—their status and sense of worth—ahead of Joseph. Reuben and Judah had each come up with schemes to rescue Joseph, but neither one had put himself between the murderous brothers and Joseph, and said "take me instead of him." But now Judah does just that on behalf of Benjamin.

Leon Kass describes Joseph's testing of his brothers in terms of Rambam's laws of *Teshuva*:

> Joseph has now decided to put his brothers to the fullest test. He will place them in a position where they will be strongly tempted to treat Benjamin as they had treated him. The point of Joseph's trial is that repentance is only complete when one knows that if he were placed in the same position he would not act in the same way he had acted before.[4]

Kass goes on to describe Judah's response to the test:

> His magnanimous and self-sacrificing offer to remain as Joseph's slave in Benjamin's stead is unparalleled in the book of Genesis; in the Torah, it is surpassed only by Moses' pleas to God to forgive Israel for the golden calf, asking to be erased from God's book should He refuse to forgive his people for their sin.[5]

In contrast with Moses in the golden-calf incident, who had not sinned at that point, Judah's "magnanimous and self-sacrificing offer" is a sign of his turnaround. He was the opposite of magnanimous and self-sacrificing when he participated in the betrayal and sale of Joseph. Now, in similar circumstances, he turns around so decisively that the whole story changes course— or flows into the course intended for it all along.

When we consider this story in real-life terms, however, we might have a problem. When someone has betrayed our trust, we might be able to forgive him, and we might even be able in time to start to trust him again. But we're unlikely to let him get into the same position where he could hurt us again, which means he never can prove how fully he's changed—which means in turn that we'll never trust him as much as we did before.

I often run into this dilemma in marriage counseling. Let's say the husband is verbally and physically abusive, so the couple finally has to separate. Once they're separated, the husband admits his problems, gets help, and is consistently pleasant and reasonable. But you don't know whether he's really turned around until he's out of the doghouse, living back at home and resuming normal life. It's only when he's back in the same situation in which he abused his wife that you'll know whether he's genuinely turned away from his abusive behavior. But, here's the dilemma: You don't want to let him get into that situation until you have solid reason to believe he's made the turnaround. Therefore, one of the essentials to restoring trust is for the offended party to identify specific, visible behaviors the offender can do to make his (or her) *teshuva* credible and trustworthy. And this requires similar circumstances to those in which the offense took place.

In our example of an abusive spouse, you're only going to know things have changed when the spouse gets into a frustrating or challenging situation, one in which he can't just glibly be on his best behavior. In other words, before the returnee gets into the position where he could commit the same exact sin again and prove himself by *not* doing it, he needs to work on some smaller proofs. He needs to not get angry when he takes his wife out for a date (even though he's still living in the doghouse) and it doesn't lead to anything beyond a goodnight peck on the cheek. He needs to not be verbally abusive when she does something he disagrees with, to not threaten physical abuse by shouting, walking out of the room when he gets frustrated, or slamming his fist down on the counter to make a point. In other words, there are signs that the returnee is ready to risk returning to the scene of the crime so he can do the right thing there.

Joseph, through his elaborate test of his brothers, is able to get them into the same position, with the same temptation, that they were in 22 years earlier, when they betrayed him. Now they renounce that betrayal, as we've seen, by taking three steps:

▶ They show authentic, articulated remorse, and confess the specifics of their wrongdoing.

▶ They take responsibility (through their representative Judah): a clear, concrete, and credible commitment to do the right thing in place of the wrong thing they did before.

▶ They pay the price (again through Judah), whatever it takes to follow through on that commitment.

▶ As a result Joseph can *extend* enough trust to reveal himself to his brothers.

Joseph speaks the unforgettable words, *"Ani Yosef, ha'od avi chai*—I am Joseph, does my father yet live?" (45:3). The brothers can't answer because they are "dismayed" or "dumfounded" at his appearance. They're standing there, jaws on the floor. So Joseph calls to them, "'Come near to me—*g'shu na elai.'* And they came near—*vayigashu*—and he said, 'I am Joseph your brother'" (45:4–5).

I'm including some of the Hebrew in this passage, and providing a literal translation, because it echoes the opening phrase of our parasha, *Vayigash elav Yehudah,* "Judah drew near to him" (44:18). The same Hebrew root—*nagash*—appears twice in 45:4–5. It's a fairly common word in the Tanakh, where it often applies to close, even intimate, and intense contact. It's actually risky to "draw near" to a ruler in this way, without being invited. But Judah takes the risk, and Joseph rewards his risky move by calling the entire family to draw near. Judah initiates reconciliation by drawing near to offer himself as a substitute for Benjamin, and Joseph completes the reconciliation by inviting his whole family to draw near. Because Judah has the courage to draw near, even at great risk to himself, Joseph can invite his whole family to draw near.

In this atmosphere of restored trust Joseph tells his brothers, "God sent me ahead of you to ensure that you will have descendants on earth and to save your lives in a great deliverance. So it was not you who sent me here, but God" (45:7–8).

In our religious communities, we speak and preach a lot about trusting God, but not so much about trusting each other. But the two are interlinked. As in Jacob's family, a breakdown of trust in others is often a symptom of breakdown of trust in God. The brothers had no sense of God's nearness and care when they plotted against Joseph, no trust that God would resolve the conflict over favor. They couldn't trust Joseph with being favored, or their father with showing his favor, because they didn't trust God. In contrast, Joseph, at some point in his long and complicated story, came to trust that God was behind it all. He trusted God behind the scenes and so he was able to extend trust to his brothers when the time came.

Still, Joseph has to put his brothers through their test because you can't restore trust by giving it blindly, any more than you can restore trust by demanding it. "Just trust me" doesn't work. But you can be ready to extend trust, and you can earn trust through your deeds. And we do both by trusting God, and taking whatever risk is necessary because we trust in him.

## Healthy differentiation

The basic relationship triangle in this whole story is Joseph-brothers-Jacob, and it's not always a healthy triangle. The brothers resented their father because of his favoritism toward Jacob, and triangulated their resentment onto Joseph himself (who as a young man seemed to be inviting resentment anyway). When they punished Joseph, they ended up by punishing their father as well, Jacob, who refused to be comforted for his loss of Joseph. Joseph in turn triangulates the ten brothers and Benjamin. That is, he doesn't relate to the ten brothers directly, but through their treatment of Benjamin. We might consider this a healthy triangulation, because Joseph refuses to resolve things with his brothers apart from Jacob (both directly and as represented by Benjamin), or to be reconciled with Jacob apart from his brothers. This triangulation will allow him to bring the whole family down to Egypt, to survive the famine and to be together at last.

Edwin Friedman emphasizes the strength and stability of the triangle, and hence its persistence, even when one is trying to change it. Ironically, after the extended 22-year drama of Joseph's exile, imprisonment and exaltation, even after his extended trial of his brothers and Judah's heroic offer of self-sacrifice, the old triangle—Jacob-Joseph-brothers—is restored. Joseph's first words when he reveals himself to his brothers include his father: "I am Joseph, does my father yet live?" In Egypt, Joseph really is the chosen one, and his relationship to his father is different from that of any other brother. But now the brothers accept this triangle, and it works to their benefit.

What has changed is that Joseph has now differentiated himself, to use Friedman's terminology, in a healthy way.

When Joseph is finally able to reveal himself to his brothers, it is clear he intends to remain connected with them. The Midrash says that when his brothers came near to him, "He showed them that he was circumcised, AND HE SAID: I AM JOSEPH YOUR BROTHER" (*Genesis Rabbah* 93:6). This interpretation sounds pretty earthy to our urban 21st-century ears, but as usual with midrash, it conveys a sharp insight. In revealing himself, Joseph becomes deeply vulnerable. He returns to the most primitive and intense level of his identity, sealed upon him when he was eight days old. He is, of course, his own man as the prime minister of Egypt. At the same time, he remains connected with his brothers, with the family of Israel, in the deepest way—so deep, in fact, that he can continue to fulfill his identity as the Egyptian prime minister without compromising the family connection.

In this scene, Joseph is indeed the hero, and the brothers do indeed bow down to him, in fulfillment of his dreams—at which they had taken such offense before (Gen. 42:9, 44:14). But Joseph's focus is no longer on himself and his position of favor. Instead, he has a clear plan to secure the future of his family, and he goes about executing that plan through the rest of our parasha, which brings us almost to the end of Genesis 47. He knows who he is, and doesn't need to flaunt it or seek affirmation from his brothers. At the same time, who he is remains deeply connected with the whole family.

This simple but powerful combination of knowing who you are individually even as you continue to belong to your family or group is the essence of self-differentiation. Rabbi Friedman sees self-differentiation as the key to successful leadership, whether of a family or a community, and highlights its three components:[6]

▶ **Stay connected.** Stay in touch. This doesn't sound so difficult (although with some families even this first step is very difficult), but is meaningful only as yoked to a second component:

▶ **Define yourself clearly.** "Take nonreactive, clearly conceived, and clearly defined positions." A feature of Joseph's test of brothers is how well-designed and executed it is, and how patient Joseph is in letting it all play out and in waiting for the right moment to reveal himself. It would have been easy to take a reactive position (in contrast with Friedman's "nonreactive" one) and punish or completely reject his brothers—or just deny their betrayal and pretend to go back to normal. A differentiated leader resists both extremes. He or she has a clear, well-defined position and sticks to it. Joseph's position throughout the entire story is to save and restore his family, and nothing knocks him off course.

▶ **Calmly handle any sabotage that results.** Friedman sees sabotage as inevitable when one family member defines himself clearly and yet stays connected. Steinke applies this truth to congregational leaders, urging them to "recognize resistance as a normal reaction to leadership rather than taking it personally."[7] Whether in family or congregation, the leader responds to such sabotage not by bullying, persuading or renegotiating, but by continuing to lead. He or she doesn't need to be rigid; he or she can change positions, *if persuaded*, so this change still represents a clearly conceived and defined position.

Joseph had experienced plenty of sabotage in his early years, but it's not clear whether it continued after he revealed himself to his brothers. They seem to fade into the background after the revelation scene, until Jacob's final blessing in Genesis 49. But the Narrator gives us two hints of an underlying tension: He mentions Reuben again as the firstborn in the list of those who came down to Egypt (46:8), and he notes Judah is appointed to lead the way to Egypt ahead of Jacob (46:28). Competition for preeminence is still in play, and even if there's no objective sabotage, Joseph needs to maintain his calm and his focus as the actual leader of his family.

## Joseph returns

Let's take a closer look at the climactic reconciliation between the brothers before we move on. In the reconciliation scene, as I said above, Joseph is the hero, and he has taken a classic hero's journey to reach this point. He started out underage and unqualified and was cast out of his homeland into exile. Like a classic hero, Joseph in Egypt experienced an ordeal of defeat and captivity, but was transformed by it and finally set free. Through it all, Joseph has a guardian, who brings him through to victory in the end—the God of his forefathers Abraham, Isaac and Jacob. And now, like a classic hero, Joseph must return home to be a source of blessing and power to his once-estranged family.

Joseph's betrayal into slavery in Egypt launched the journey, and he brings it home when he reveals himself to the brothers who betrayed him. He can't return to the Promised Land yet, but he reunites with his brothers, describes his plan to save them from the famine, and concludes, "and bring my father here with all speed." His journey won't be over until he's reunited with his father. "Then he embraced his brother Binyamin and wept, and Binyamin wept on his neck, and he kissed all his brothers and wept on them. After that, his brothers talked with him" (45:14-15).

So far the brothers have not uttered a word. It is only after this emotional embrace that their consternation is overcome. They are now able to communicate with Joseph, something they were unable to do when he lived among them as a boy.[8]

The brothers are being healed of an estrangement that goes back to their earliest years. Joseph, the hero who has returned, is able to bring healing to the broken family of Jacob.

At the same time, Joseph continues with his trust-building test. He "kissed all his brothers," but he had embraced Benjamin first. Furthermore, "To each of them he gave a set of new clothes; but to Binyamin he gave seven-and-a-half pounds of silver and five sets of new clothes" (45:22). We're reminded that the remedy for the competition for favor is *not* to eliminate favor itself. It's part of real-life human relationships that there will be degrees and differences of love and favor. One lesson of our story—counter-cultural indeed in our day of boundless inclusivity—is to accept and embrace one's place within the extended family or community system, not comparing it with the place of others, and even to support the favor another family member might receive. Joseph wants to make sure his brothers can now support Jacob's favor toward Benjamin. And just in case the brothers don't get this lesson, as they're about to return to Canaan to regather their households and their father, Joseph admonishes them, "Don't quarrel among yourselves while you're traveling!" (45:24).

## Recognition and rescue

We've already considered Joseph as a forerunner or sign of a Messiah to come, and the rabbinic discussion of Mashiach ben Yosef, Messiah the son of Joseph. Joseph is rejected by his brothers, sold into slavery among the Gentiles, buried in a dungeon, and finally raised up again to be the source of salvation for Israel and all the nations. But on the way to saving his people, Joseph hides his identity from his own family. When the sons of Israel appear before Joseph in Egypt, he recognizes his brothers but they don't recognize him (Gen. 42:8). *The Voice of the Turtledove*, a rabbinic study of Mashiach ben Yosef, discusses this theme of postponed recognition:

> This is one of the traits of Joseph not only in his own generation, but in every generation, i.e., that Mashiach ben Yosef recognizes his brothers, but they do not recognize him. This is the work of Satan, who hides the characteristics of Mashiach ben Yosef so that the footsteps of the Mashiach are not recognized and are even belittled because of our many sins. . . . Were Israel to recognize Joseph, that is, the footsteps of ben Yosef the Mashiach which is the ingathering of the exiles, etc., then we would already have been redeemed with a complete redemption.[9]

Another rabbinic commentary sees Joseph's revelation of himself to his brothers as a sign of the deliverance to come.

> When Joseph said, "I am Joseph," God's master plan became clear to the brothers. They had no more questions. Everything that had happened for the last twenty-two years fell into perspective. So, too, will it be in the time to come, when God will reveal Himself and announce, "I am Hashem!" The veil will be lifted from our eyes and we will comprehend everything that has transpired throughout history (*Chafetz Chaim*).[10]

When the rabbis speak of the unrecognized Messiah, they are not at all thinking of Yeshua, Jesus of Nazareth. Yet it's remarkable how closely Yeshua's story aligns with Joseph's story and the portrayal of Messiah ben Joseph. Yeshua is rejected by his brothers, cast out from the household of Israel, given over to death under the dominant Gentile power, and then raised from the dead. He becomes the source of salvation to the nations, while his own nation, Israel, cannot recognize him. Yeshua's identity is cloaked by his sojourn in the Gentile world, as Joseph's was cloaked by his high position in the court of Egypt. He speaks a language his brothers cannot understand, though he understands theirs. For his hero's journey to be complete, however, he must return home and be reunited with his brothers.

The rejection by (most of) Israel and the failure of (most of) Israel to recognize Yeshua as their own deliverer becomes the source of salvation to the nations, as Paul notes in his letter to the Romans:

> "In that case, I say, isn't it that [the people of Israel] have stumbled with the result that they have permanently fallen away?" Heaven forbid! Quite the contrary, it is by means of their stumbling that the deliverance has come to the Gentiles, in order to provoke them to jealousy. (Rom. 11:11)

It's just a step from there to the idea, captured in the rabbinic texts above, that Israel's recognition of Messiah ben Joseph will bring redemption to both Israel and the nations. "For if their casting Yeshua aside means reconciliation for the world, what will their accepting him mean? It will be life from the dead!" (Rom. 11:15).

For many of us in the Messianic Jewish community, our initial encounter with Yeshua as Messiah launched a journey away from our Jewish homes and family, a journey that often included testing and estrangement. But for this to be a hero's journey like that of Joseph or even Messiah himself, it must include a return to our Jewish household. Whatever rescue and transformation we've received from God should issue forth in blessing for our people. So it was with Joseph, who told his brothers,

> "But don't be sad that you sold me into slavery here or angry at yourselves, because it was God who sent me ahead of you to preserve life. . . . God sent me ahead of you to ensure that you will have descendants on earth and to save your lives in a great deliverance. So it was not you who sent me here, but God." (45:5, 7–8a)

Like Joseph, Yeshua is estranged from his own brothers, the household of Israel, yet as with Joseph, his heart is always with them. It's a needed reminder in this day of individualism and autonomy. Joseph cannot and will not complete his hero's journey apart from his brothers, and neither will Messiah himself. And so we who follow him need to remain firmly connected to his people and their destiny. This parallel also reminds us that our individual journey can't reach its destination by simply departing from our family of origin. We may need to do hard and sacrificial work to stay connected, and may not be able to fix all that's wrong in our family, but we can't altogether depart. In my experience as a therapist, I've learned it's often the client who appears to be the most distant from his or her family that is carrying the heaviest load of family baggage wherever they go. We can't take a detour around forgiveness and reconciliation.

## Reunited with the father

Joseph's self-revelation to his brothers opens the way for him to be reunited with his father Jacob. As I noted earlier, we often call this entire section of Genesis (chapters 37 through 50) the Joseph story, but, as Jeffrey Feinberg notes, "Perhaps it really is a story about Ya'akov's legacy to his sons."[11] Of the four parashiyot that make up this story, two—the first and the last—have Jacob as their subject: *Vayeshev*, "and he [Jacob] dwelt," and *Vayechi*, "and he [Jacob] lived." In the first parasha, "even as Ya'akov tries to dig in and settle down in the Land God has sworn to give him, his family fragments and begins to assimilate."[12] Ironically, it's in Egypt, a land of exile, that the family becomes whole again. There Jacob will return to center stage in the family drama, illustrating another principle of family dynamics. In a healthy family, the parents take the central role. In the ancient world of the Bible, the father normally was the representative parent. As Jacob's sons come into order, he can regain his position as father, and the family can move away from fragmentation and assimilation to wholeness. Jacob's desires as a father are no longer being resisted and thwarted by his offspring, and as a result the whole family can take a deep breath and begin to prosper in the land of Egypt.

When I say Jacob returns to center stage, however, you might notice he doesn't seem to do a whole lot in this part of the story. Actually, though, Jacob doesn't need to do a lot to foster the healing Judah and Joseph have initiated. What he does need to do is simply to be present, to be engaged and in close touch with his family, and this calm presence will be sufficient. This is what Rabbi Friedman describes as "maintaining a nonanxious presence" in the midst of the family or congregation (or organization) that one leads.[13] A calm, present leader, Friedman claims, reduces tension and anxiety throughout the whole family or congregation, so all the members are free to relate and function in healthier ways.

Jacob's family, even after the reunion with Joseph, is undoubtedly still loaded with anxiety: Will they really survive the famine? Who will take over when Jacob is gone? Since Judah took the lead in reuniting the family and transferring them down to Egypt (46:28), and Joseph has taken the lead in Egypt, who is really in charge here? Will Joseph really forgive his brothers and treat them well, or is he just making nice until Jacob dies?[14] Will Pharaoh genuinely accept them and treat them with dignity?

Amid such questions, Jacob had already responded with great simplicity and calm, "Enough! My son Yosef is still alive! I must go and see him before I die" (45:28). The Narrator continues, "So Israel took his journey with all that he had" (46:1, ESV). Jacob doesn't exhort his sons or question how it is that Joseph is still alive, after they had brought his bloodied tunic to him so many years before. He simply leads out. But then the caravan pauses in Beersheba to offer sacrifices to God. Beersheba is on the way to Egypt, but only about twenty-five miles from the region of Hebron, their likely starting-point. What is the reason for this final stop before taking the long journey through the Sinai desert to Egypt? Nahum Sarna notes that the journey itself, especially for one of Jacob's advanced age, "would be an understandable cause of great anxiety."

But verse 3 shows that Jacob's doubt and hesitation go much deeper. Is the patriarch distressed at having to leave the promised land? Is he afraid of dying on alien soil? Are his fears intensified by the memory that his father had been expressly forbidden by God to go to Egypt (26:2)? Perhaps he is troubled by the recollection of the divine announcement to Abraham that his descendants were destined to be enslaved and oppressed as strangers in a foreign land (15:13). At any rate, Jacob seems to experience a sudden reluctance to continue the journey.[15]

Does Jacob lose the "nonanxious presence" he seems to have in 45:28? If so, God restores his calm. He appears to Jacob in visions of the night, confirms his direction, and promises to bring his people back from Egypt to the Promised Land. And then, "Jacob set out from Beersheba. The sons of Israel carried Jacob their father" (46:5 ESV). The Hebrew word translated "set out" is *va-yakom*, which is usually followed by an action. Abimelech and Phicol "set out" and return to the land of the Philistines (21:32). Abraham's servant "sets out" and goes to Aram-naharaim (24:1). But here, Sarna notes, the term "signifies firm resolve. The action is performed by his sons because Jacob is too weak."[16] Jacob no longer has much vitality or strength, but he now has vision and resolve, which he bears with his nonanxious presence—and that's enough to mobilize his sons to return to Egypt and carry him down.

## Jacob blesses Pharaoh

After the family of Jacob arrives in Egypt, Joseph reports to Pharaoh and presents a few of his brothers to him. Then he brings Jacob and presents him separately (47:7ff.), probably to honor his father by giving him his own audience with the king. The Narrator says, "And Jacob blessed Pharaoh." This can be translated, as in the JPS TANAKH, "and Jacob greeted Pharaoh," but "blessed" would be the more-usual translation for the Hebrew term, *va-yevarekh*, from the root *barakh*. Even if the term in this immediate context simply means "greeted," however, the actual language reminds us of the theme of blessing that runs throughout Genesis. This theme appears at the very beginning of the story of Abraham and his family.

> Now *Adonai* said to Avram, "Get yourself out of your country, away from your kinsmen and away from your father's house, and go to the land that I will show you. I will make of you a great nation, I will *bless* you, and I will make your name great; and you are to be a *blessing*. I will *bless* those who *bless* you, but I will curse anyone who curses you; and by you all the families of the earth will be *blessed*." (12:1–3, emphasis added)

"Bless/blessing" appears five times in this brief passage, alerting us that it will be a dominant theme in the story to follow. The blessing will be passed on from generation to generation in the line of Abraham, Isaac and Jacob. The promise of becoming a blessing to all the families of the earth is confirmed to Abraham (22:18) and repeated to Isaac (26:4) and to Jacob (28:14). Finally, when Jacob meets with Pharaoh in our parasha, his blessing on Pharaoh anticipates the promise of blessing upon all nations, here represented by Egypt, the greatest nation of the biblical world. The story had already hinted at this blessing earlier, when Joseph was a bondservant in the house of Potiphar. "From the time he appointed him manager of his household and all his possessions, Adonai *blessed* the Egyptian's household for Yosef's sake; Adonai's *blessing* was on all he owned, whether in the house or in the field" (39:5, emphasis added). Just to make sure we get this connection, the Narrator frames Jacob's whole encounter with Pharaoh with the blessing: "Jacob blessed Pharaoh" upon his arrival (v. 7), and "Jacob blessed Pharaoh" (the identical wording in Hebrew in v. 10), upon his departure.

Jacob really doesn't need to do more than to appear and speak this simple word of blessing. Again we see the power of presence, so evident in family dynamics, the power a parent or leader has to impart blessing, encouragement and vision if he or she simply remains present and engaged, stays above all the anxieties and tensions, and speaks a simple word when needed.

## Joseph serves Pharaoh

Before we conclude this parasha and move on to the final installment of our story, we'll turn our attention to an aspect of the tale that we might find troubling. Joseph's service to Pharaoh reflects the way he had served his father years before. He was totally devoted to his father, even at times at the expense of his brothers. The young Joseph seemed clueless about the danger of stirring up their resentment because of his favored position (e.g. 37:4–5, 9, 14). In a similar way, Joseph is so devoted to Pharaoh that he uses the occasion of the famine to purchase all the land of Egypt for him, and make all the residents of the land servants of Pharaoh (47:20–26), without much apparent regard for his "brothers," the other subjects of Pharaoh. He seems to assume everyone will be just fine with this new arrangement.

As I noted in our first chapter, the role of number-two man or woman, who is so loyal to the master and so capable that the master can entrust everything to him or her, fits the later-born better than the firstborn. The firstborn, in contrast, is eager to make his own way, and might see service to the father or master mostly as a means to the end of taking over himself someday. Joseph doesn't appear to have that agenda, which is why his father and Pharaoh—and Potiphar and the keeper of the prison as well—can entrust everything to him. What might be troubling to us, though, is that Joseph is so loyal to Pharaoh that he acquires all the land of Egypt, and even all the people of Egypt, as property of the crown. From our 21st-century perspective, Joseph might look like an instrument of oppression and injustice. But the Egyptians, whose lives he has saved, see it differently, and tell Joseph, "You have saved our lives! So if it pleases my lord, we will be Pharaoh's slaves" (47:25). Apparently Joseph is right to assume everyone will be fine with his new arrangement. Nahum Sarna explains,

> Memories of the African slave trade color our view of slavery, so that we cannot understand this expression of gratitude. But in ancient society slavery was the accepted way of bailing out the destitute, and under a benevolent master could be quite a comfortable status (cf. Joseph with Potiphar).[17]

Of course, the family of Jacob will come to experience a much darker side of slavery later in Egypt, and the theme of liberation will become dominant in the writings of the biblical prophets, forming a vision of freedom that has persisted until our day. Even the Midrash will question Joseph's policy of taxing the Egyptians at twenty percent, or one-fifth of their produce.

> Pharaoh owned nothing of the world, yet Joseph ordered, AND IT SHALL COME TO PASS AT THE INGATHERINGS, THAT YE SHALL GIVE A FIFTH UNTO PHARAOH. But the Holy One, blessed be He, to whom belongs everything, commands thee to separate to Him only one tenth! (*Genesis Rabbah* 95)

The arrangement isn't fair by the standards to be created in the Hebrew Bible, but it is a life-saver to the desperate Egyptians. It also takes the form of a relational triangle, which is normally stable and hard to disrupt.

Joseph had created a healthy triangulation by placing himself between Pharaoh and his family. He told his brothers to tell

Pharaoh they were "keepers of livestock," as their ancestors had been, because shepherds were abhorrent to the Egyptians. In gratitude to Joseph, Pharaoh will let his family settle in Egypt, but because they follow a despised trade, he'll keep them separated in the district of Goshen, exactly where Joseph wanted them to settle (46:34–47:6)! Joseph leverages his relationship to both Pharaoh and his own family in ways that reconcile both and allow their harmonious cohabitation in Egypt. The triangulation he creates between himself, Pharaoh and the Egyptian people seems equally benign and lasts until the conclusion of Genesis. Somewhere along the way, however, both triangles shift and the sons of Israel will be reduced to slavery, as the Pharaohs forget the great benefit Joseph had brought them. Exodus continues the story: "Now there arose a new king over Egypt. He knew nothing about Yosef" (Ex 1:8).

Before we get there, however, we need to hear the rest of the tale of Joseph and his brothers, and especially the culmination of the story of Jacob, and how he resolves the rivalry for favor among his sons. That will be the theme of our next parasha.

# Chapter Four

# *Vayechi*
# "And he lived"

*Ya'akov lived in the land of Egypt seventeen years;*
*thus Ya'akov lived to be 147 years old.*

Joseph asked in the last parasha, "Is my father still alive?"
Now in our final parasha, the opening word is *Vayechi*, "And he
lived."

We've been following our story as the account of Joseph and
his brothers, but to Joseph it's all about his father, Jacob.
Joseph's miraculous rise in Egypt from bondage to lordship
means little to him if he can't see his father's face one more time.
And if we're paying attention to the story, we'll come to share
that perspective. Joseph is a hero, and so is Judah, but the story is
ultimately about Jacob, the father, and his love for a favored son.

Our concluding parasha will tell of the deaths of Jacob and
Joseph, yet its title, *Vayechi*, puts the focus not on death, but on
life; not on the past, but on the future of Israel. Both Jacob and
Joseph look toward the future as they approach the moment of
death, and they approach death itself with calm reliance on the
Almighty.

# A good death

Among the many things we've lost in our techno-materialistic, secular age is the art of dying well. In past centuries, a good death was considered the culmination of a good life. George Washington, for example, perhaps with a premonition of his coming death, drafted a new will in the summer of 1799, writing out its twenty-nine pages by hand. He divided his estate among fifty family members, and made detailed provisions for the freedom and support of his slaves after his death, including the highly unusual order that his young slaves who were to be freed "be taught to read and write and to be brought up to some useful occupation."[1] When the moment of death arrived just a few months later, Washington told his lifelong friend Dr. Craik, who was attending him, "Doctor, I die hard, but I am not afraid to go."[2] His confidence was undoubtedly based on his belief in Providence, which, as he'd written in a letter two years earlier, "has directed my steps and shielded me in the various changes and chances through which I have passed from my youth to the present moment."[3]

Consciously or not, Washington, and countless others like him, were following the example of our spiritual predecessors, who focused with calm assurance on the future, not the past, and on passing on their legacy, as they approached the moment of death. The person of faith doesn't limit his gaze to his own lifespan, or to his share in eternal bliss to come; rather, even in his final moments, he continues to look and prepare the way toward the future for those he will leave behind.

We can trace this quality in the life of Jacob. When he first arrived in Egypt, Joseph presented him before Pharaoh, who asked him, "'How old are you?' and Ya'akov replied, 'The time of my stay on earth has been 130 years; they have been few and difficult, fewer than the years my ancestors lived.' Then Ya'akov blessed Pharaoh and left his presence" (47:8–10). Here Jacob is looking back, and isn't too happy with what he sees. Seventeen years later, however, when he reaches the end of his earthly sojourn, he looks ahead, first bestowing a double blessing upon Joseph, through adopting his two sons Ephraim and Manasseh (chapter 48), then telling all his sons, "Gather yourselves together, and I will tell you / what will happen to you in the *acharit-hayamim*" ("the last days" or simply "the days to come"; chapter 49). Only after he outlines the future of each of his sons does Jacob look to his own future, which will entail being gathered to his ancestors, who are entombed in the Promised Land.

Before we consider some elements of chapters 48 and 49 in detail, let's return to the opening verse of our parasha, "Ya'akov lived in the land of Egypt seventeen years" (47:28). The whole saga of the generations of Jacob, the story of Joseph and his brothers, opens when Joseph is seventeen years old (37:2). These two seventeen-year periods bookend the entire story and highlight how Jacob's life "had been wholly intertwined with that of Joseph."[4] Jacob's life has come full-circle, and despite the bitter rivalry of Joseph's brothers and 22 years of estrangement, Joseph remains at the center of that circle.

This fact highlights two family dynamics evident in this story. First is the persistence of the inherited narrative and the roles that family members play within it. Each member finds or is assigned his or her place in the family system, and it becomes difficult to change that place, even after decades, and even after death. This persistence of roles is evident in families today. The schoolgirl who becomes the family hero because of her straight-A performance in class remains the family hero into midlife and beyond. The scapegoat who was loaded down with all the frustrations and failures of his alcoholic father remains the scapegoat long after the father has died. Likewise, with Jacob, after years of separation it's still all about Joseph, the family hero.

We can waste a lot of time and generate a lot of frustration trying to change habits and attitudes within our families or congregations (or any group we're involved in) if we don't pay attention to the inherited narrative and the family roles within it. On the other hand, if we do recognize the roles individual members are filling, we can sometimes help modify or adjust those roles in significant ways. The family hero can fail to function in some small regard and cause a realignment in the way the whole family operates. The scapegoat can learn to walk away from the cycle of blame and shame he's caught in, and cause the whole family to readjust. Judah's move away from disgruntled rival to self-sacrificing big brother shifted the dynamic of the entire family of Jacob.

## Ephraim and Manasseh

The second family dynamic is related to the first. Family roles don't easily change, and neither do family attitudes and habits. Jacob in his final years still has his favorites. But with wisdom we can recognize the strength within these attitudes and habits, which seem negative at first, rather than trying to change them altogether.

So, as his death approaches, Jacob reaffirms his favor toward Joseph by raising up Joseph's two sons, Ephraim and Manasseh, to the same status as his own twelve sons. "Now your two sons, who were born to you in the land of Egypt before I came to you in Egypt, are mine; Efrayim and M'nasheh will be as much mine as Re'uven and Shim'on are" (48:5). And even after this move,

Jacob still elevates one of the two sons of Joseph over the other. Joseph places Ephraim and Manasseh before Jacob to receive their blessings, according to birth order:

> Efrayim in his right hand toward Isra'el's left hand and M'nasheh in his left hand toward Isra'el's right hand. . . . But Isra'el put out his right hand and laid it on the head of the younger one, Efrayim, and put his left hand on the head of M'nasheh—he intentionally crossed his hands, even though M'nasheh was the firstborn. (48:13–14)

As he had done with Joseph, Jacob is again reversing the usual order of things to favor the later-born over the firstborn—a reflection of God's own prerogative of choosing the younger, the weaker, the lowly and unrecognized, to accomplish his purposes. Ironically, Joseph, who benefited from such a reversal when he received status that arguably belonged to an older brother, objects to this reversal of status when it happens to his two sons.

> When Yosef saw that his father was laying his right hand on Efrayim's head, it displeased him, and he lifted up his father's hand to remove it from Efrayim's head and place it instead on M'nasheh's head. Yosef said to his father, "Don't do it that way, my father; for this one is the firstborn. Put your right hand on his head." (48:13)

Jacob assures Joseph he knows what he is doing, perhaps in response to the implication that he's old and infirm and just made an old man's mistake.

> But his father refused and said, "I know that, my son, I know it. He too will become a people, and he too will be great; nevertheless his younger brother will be greater than he, and his descendants will grow into many nations." (48:14)

Ephraim and Manasseh are the final pair in the long series of brother-rivals for status in the book of Genesis. There's a difference with them, however, that we shouldn't overlook, as my colleague David Wein notes:

> This time there is no supplanting going on, none of the trickery and fraternal rivalry that we've seen in Jacob's narrative (or in the greater narrative of the patriarchs in Genesis). We remember Cain and Abel, Isaac and Ishmael, Jacob and Esau, Joseph and his brothers. Even the "sister wives" conflicts can be seen this way: Sarah and Hagar, Rachel and Leah. But Ephraim and Manasseh are different. There is no record of their rivalry in the text. This seems to be a break from the cycle of brother against brother, pointing toward humility, harmony, and preferring the other to themselves.[5]

Here is another hint at boundless favor, the recognition that there's enough favor to go around, that if someone gets a bigger share of favor it doesn't deprive me . . . and may even turn out to be a source of blessing for me.

Underlying Jacob's evident favoritism, which is deeply engrained and unlikely to change, is his prophetic sense of God's purposes. If we focus on how unfair the favoritism is, or wish we could change it, we not only ignore the power of long-term family patterns, but we might also reject the profound insights behind the favoritism. It's good to work for fairness and right order, but God can work behind the scenes, despite the unfairness and disorder, to accomplish a good result for everyone involved. Jacob, with all his flaws and inconsistencies, has a unique ability to recognize what God is up to.

As we continue to examine the story of Jacob and his sons, we realize that family dynamics alone can't explain everything.

God has a deeper purpose. In the same way, as we gain understanding of the dynamics of our own families and congregations (and other organizations as well), we still need to discern God's purposes behind the familial tensions and misunderstandings. Rigid adherence to "the way it's always been done," like Joseph's objection to the reversed blessing on Ephraim and Manasseh, can miss what God is doing among us. And sometimes, the one who is the most rigid about the way things should be done is someone, like Joseph, who once benefited from a reversal of the status quo. Family dynamics might be dysfunctional, but wisdom is alert to God's redemptive activity behind it all.

## The blessing on Judah

Sometime after Jacob blesses his two grandsons, he blesses his twelve sons. It's beyond the scope of this book to cover Jacob's blessing in its entirety, but it's important to note that all the sons are present together to receive blessing from their father. The whole chapter of blessing opens as "Ya'akov called for [all] his sons and said,

> "Gather yourselves together, and I will tell you what will happen to you in the *acharit-hayamim*. Assemble yourselves and listen, sons of Ya'akov; pay attention to Isra'el your father." (49:1–2)

These words emphasize (at last) the wholeness and inclusiveness of the family. We get a glimpse of the family itself as the place of favor and blessing upon all its members, with the competition for favor and blessing no longer relevant. This is the atmosphere children long for in their families, that members long for in a religious community—an atmosphere of boundless favor and unconditional inclusion. But, just as in the story of Ephraim and

Manasseh in chapter 48, the text here only hints at this atmosphere of peace, and soon the drama of birth order and rivalry begins to play out again within the blessing itself. Since this particular drama has two heroes, Judah and Joseph, we'll look at the blessing that Jacob gives to each of them, with a focus on the sibling rivalry between them, and how Jacob brings that to resolution.

The blessing on Judah opens with a clear statement of his preeminence:

> Y'hudah, your brothers will acknowledge you,
> your hand will be on the neck of your enemies,
> your father's sons will bow down before you. (49:8)

Notice the word "bow" or "bow down" here. We've already seen it several times in this story.[6] In Joseph's early dreams, the brothers' sheaves of grain *bow down* before his sheaf, and the sun, moon and eleven stars *bow down* before Joseph, so that his father rebukes him: "What is this dream you have dreamed? Am I and your mother and your brothers really going to come and *bow down* before you on the ground?" (37:7–10, literal translation). The answer to Jacob's question finally begins to emerge many years later, when Joseph becomes governor of the land of Egypt, and his brothers come and *bow down* before him on the ground (42:6, 43:26). In his final blessing, though, Jacob reverses this pattern to declare that it is to *Judah* the brothers will finally bow.

In his series of blessings, Jacob had already passed over his firstborn, Reuben, who was unstable, and had defiled his father's bed by sleeping with his concubine (49:3–4). The two sons who were next in line, Simeon and Levi, had also disqualified themselves because of the violence and cruelty they displayed in the matter of Shechem and Dinah (49:5–7; cf.

Gen. 34). Preeminence finally comes to rest upon Judah, then, not just because he's next in line, but arguably, because he has demonstrated his worthiness. By offering himself in exchange for Benjamin, he triggered the reconciliation with Joseph, as we saw in our last chapter. Joseph, the favored younger son, had seemed on course to rule over the sons of Israel throughout the story. But now,

> Everyone hears it from Jacob himself that Judah is to replace Joseph as the first among equals. Joseph, it appears, had only half understood his youthful "Egyptian" dream about the sheaves of wheat; his brothers did indeed bow down to him, but only in Egypt. In Israel, his brothers—including Joseph's sons—will be led by Judah.[7]

Judah's leadership, however, is not that of an ordinary firstborn. As we saw earlier, in the story of Judah and Tamar, the line of Messiah will come through him. Jacob affirms this promise in his blessing:

> Y'hudah is a lion's cub;
> my son, you stand over the prey.
> He crouches down and stretches like a lion;
> like a lioness, who dares to provoke him?
> The scepter will not pass from Y'hudah,
> nor the ruler's staff from between his legs,
> until he comes to whom [obedience] belongs;
> and it is he whom the peoples will obey. (49:9–10)

The *Complete Jewish Bible* provides an alternate translation: "The scepter will not pass from Y'hudah, nor the ruler's staff from between his legs, until Shiloh comes" (footnote to verse 10). This translation closely reflects the Hebrew wording, and in my opinion is preferable. It simply reads "Shiloh" as a proper name, perhaps related to the word *shalom*, which means "peace." Many of the early Jewish commentators accepted this translation and even read "Shiloh" as a name of the Messiah. As I noted in my book *Gateways to Torah*:

> *Genesis Rabbah* states "This phrase ['until Shiloh comes'] alludes to the royal Messiah" (*Genesis Rabbah* 98.8). Rashi says Shiloh is "Messiah the king, for the kingdom is his (SHELO)." He goes on to cite Onkelos, who paraphrased the Torah in the Aramaic language years before the appearance of Yeshua the Messiah. Onkelos also interprets *Shiloh* as Messiah. Finally, the Talmud refers to this same phrase to answer the question, "What is the Messiah's name? – The school of R. Shila said: His name is Shiloh, for it is written, *until Shiloh come*" (Sanhedrin 98b).[8]

Back in Genesis 38, Judah became the father of Peretz and Zerach, and Peretz is identified in the book of Ruth as an ancestor of King David (Ruth 4:18–22), who in turn is an ancestor of the Messiah, the Son of David. In Genesis 44, Judah stepped forward to offer himself as a slave instead of his brother, anticipating the servant of Isaiah 53 who offers himself to bear the sufferings of others. Sanhedrin 98b, the same Talmudic passage referenced above, cites Isaiah 53 in discussing the name of Messiah: "The Rabbis said: His name is 'the leper scholar,' as it is written, Surely he hath borne our griefs, and carried our sorrows: yet we did esteem him a leper, smitten of God, and afflicted [Isaiah 53:4]." Now, in Genesis 49, Judah is given the scepter of Shiloh, referring to the rule of Messiah to come, who will be called the Lion of the Tribe of Judah (Rev. 5:5 cf. Gen 49:8).

# The blessing on Joseph

As we have already noted, however, the Messiah is also called Son of Joseph, and some of the rabbinic sages discuss a distinct Messiah ben Joseph who appears on the scene before Messiah ben David. In Genesis, both Judah and Joseph save their family in different ways, and both are seen as prototypes of Messiah. So before we look at some of the specifics of Jacob's final blessing upon Joseph, we should note that this shared Messiah-ship, which can seem ambiguous or confusing, is actually an essential part of the story. It can help resolve the whole problem of sibling rivalry and become a source of healing for the fragmentation this rivalry so often causes. Judah and Joseph are both favored with a unique family role, and these roles are complementary, not competing. Both sons are prototypes of a Messiah to come, and both are dedicated to the same purpose, serving the same extended family. In Jacob's family, favor is not a zero-sum commodity, so that if one member gets it, all the rest are deprived. Rather, favor is a boundless source of blessing and strength for the family, which *increases* when more than one member possesses it. In God's economy favor is without limit, and when it is divided up, it multiplies.

It can be so in our families and in our communities as well. As parents and leaders, we don't want to emulate Jacob's favoritism. Instead, his favoritism provides a sort of *qal v'homer* or "light and heavy" argument. If Jacob's sons are expected to affirm and support his love for Joseph (and later for Benjamin), even when it's expressed with such open favoritism, how much more we are to affirm and support God's special love and favor upon his people Israel, which is not merely human favoritism. We don't want to emulate Jacob's favoritism, but we do want to emulate his understanding that the favor shown to one is meant to be a source of blessing to all. We can model and teach our children or those in our extended community to affirm the good that happens to others, and not to covet it for themselves. When oldest brother Dave receives an acceptance letter from Harvard, we can help his siblings celebrate with him and relieve them of the expectation that they need to match his feat. When our friend Rebecca sings a beautiful solo or delivers a home-run Torah commentary at services, we can affirm her and the gift God has given her and not succumb to the pressure to produce something even better. We can show that life is ultimately not about competition for favor or status, but about discovering and honoring the unique assignment and boundless favor God has given each one.

From this perspective, although Joseph's blessing comes after Judah's and seems to compete with it, we can read it instead as complementary, with both blessings reflecting the same purposeful goodness of God.

The Hebrew of Joseph's blessing is difficult, and translations into English vary quite a bit. The most important part of the blessing for our discussion, however, is the conclusion, so we'll focus just on that. Jacob assures Joseph that the "Mighty One of Jacob," "the God of your father," will help him, and Shaddai, the God of the patriarchs, will bless him . . .

> with blessings from heaven above, blessings from the deep, lying below, blessings from the breasts and the womb. The blessings of your father [that is, of Jacob] are more powerful than the blessings of my parents [that is, of Abraham and Isaac], extending to the farthest of the everlasting hills; they will be on the head of Yosef, on the brow of the prince among his brothers. (49:25–26)

Judah has been given preeminence among his brothers, and yet Joseph is blessed beyond measure. Judah is heir to the blessings of Abraham, Isaac and Jacob, and yet Joseph's blessing is "more powerful." Judah has been granted the scepter of kingly rule, yet Joseph is "the prince among his brothers."

Whether these blessings are competing or complementary, however, we might well ask how they resolve—or fail to resolve—the tension between Judah and Joseph. But perhaps the Torah purposefully leaves this ambiguity in place to underscore the idea that the father's favor is not a zero-sum game. One being chosen doesn't always mean another is rejected. As we saw earlier, all the brothers are present at the scene of Jacob's blessing. That Judah and Joseph both partake of a special blessing without diminishing the other provides a hint that all the brothers will partake of blessing, even though two of them receive special favor.

Jewish theologian Michael Wyschogrod points the way beyond the competition for favor that has taken center stage throughout Genesis:

> Surely non-election does not equal rejection. Ishmael and Esau, the sons of non-election, are suffused in the divine word with a compassion in some respects more powerful than the love of the sons of election. Is it not possible that those who love God so much that, even in their non-election, they submit with love and serenity to the destiny chosen for them by God, are very dear to him indeed? Not to be the favorite son of a human father is a painful experience, but the non-election of God is never a finality, only one way of being touched by the finger of God.[9]

A Gentile who is a Christian might not speak "with love of his non-election," because he believes he is chosen in Messiah Yeshua. But he is still not part of the chosen nation, Israel. Instead, he is chosen in Messiah Yeshua as representative of a non-chosen people, and this chosenness doesn't diminish that of Israel as a people. He can "submit with love and serenity to the destiny chosen for [him as a Gentile] by God," and at the same time honor the unique destiny of Israel, the Jewish people. Our focus right now, however, is not on Jewish-Christian relations, but on the theme of favor in the story of Jacob's family, and Wyschogrod's insight is invaluable. God's favor upon one doesn't mean rejection of the other. God bestows favor, but doesn't practice favoritism.

Building on Wyschogrod's work, another Jewish scholar, Joel S. Kaminsky, discerns three categories in the family stories of Genesis; the elect, the non-elect and the anti-elect. The anti-elect were enemies of Israel and of God, but the "non-elect peoples were always considered fully part of the divine economy, and in a very real sense, Israel was to work out her destiny in relation to them." [10] Kaminsky believes the biblical doctrine of election, which is hard enough for many to accept in our postmodern culture, is made even harder by imagining that all those who are not elect, or not favored, are thereby the anti-elect. But the choice of one doesn't mean the rejection of all the rest. In the sibling rivalries of Genesis, with all their competition for the blessing, "one discovers that often the non-elect also receive some form of blessing. Furthermore, the blessing of the non-elect is frequently brought about by their relationship to the elect." [11] This is certainly the case in the story of Joseph and his brothers.

Accordingly, when Judah is chosen (49:10), Joseph is by no means rejected. Both Judah and Joseph remain favored ones, the elect of the father, and their respective elections are not mutually exclusive. On one level their elections remain in tension, only to be resolved in the end of time, when the division between Judah and Joseph (Ephraim) will be resolved at last (as in Ezek. 37). On another level, however, they serve to demonstrate that God's election is not a zero-sum game. God's favor is boundless, and it can rest upon more than one child at a time, indeed upon all his children at the same time.

Jacob refrains from resolving the Judah-Joseph tension in his final blessing, and thereby points the way beyond the sibling rivalry for favor. They are both favored: both Judah, one who gains the firstborn privilege by default; and Joseph, who is later-born and not entitled to that privilege at all. "The Joseph story brings Genesis to closure by showing that sibling rivalry is not written indelibly into the human script."[12] Instead, the ancient sibling rivalry for favor is disarmed in the presence of the God of Israel, if we understand him correctly. Jacob's final prophetic word over all his sons has the power to transform not only his family, but every family that is centered on the God of Israel. It even has the power to transform the extended family of God's people, comprising the children of Israel and the multinational assembly of Messiah Yeshua, Jews and Christians. We'll discuss this transformation in our next chapter. But first, we must attend to the final scenes in the story of Joseph and his brothers.

## The Death of Jacob

Joanne was a member of our congregation in Albuquerque years ago. She was the youngest of four children and the only one who stayed in her home town as an adult. After her father died, Joanne, who had divorced years earlier and never remarried, moved in with her aging mother to help with her care. She didn't mind, because she'd always been close to her mother.

Jason, Suzanne, and Heather, her out-of-town siblings, supported the move, and thanked Joanne for providing so much care for their mother. But as time went on, and Joanne's mother's health deteriorated, she heard less and less from her siblings. They'd do the usual holiday phone calls and greetings, and that was about it. Finally, Joanne's mother passed away after a long struggle with a blood disorder. Jason, Suzanne, and Heather all showed up for the funeral with their spouses—and they all stuck around for a few days afterwards to wonder if their mother could have lived longer with better care. They bombarded Joanne with questions about why she hadn't checked out this or that physician or clinic, and whether their mother really had that rare blood disorder in the first place. They weren't too happy about the funeral arrangements either. Joanne was devastated. She had to deal not only with the loss of her beloved mother, but with the distrust and rudeness of her brother and sisters.

When a patriarch or matriarch dies, regardless of the circumstances, the family system often becomes imbalanced. It's not unusual for family members to react erratically. The death of a father or mother figure often stirs up fighting and misunderstanding between the survivors. They might seem to be arguing over the funeral arrangements or the division of property, but the real issues are far deeper. Underlying the conflict are not only feelings of incomprehensible loss and guilt or regret, but often terror at death itself.

As a rabbi and counselor, I've learned to tread softly through the scene of grief and mourning. Joanne's case isn't the only time I've seen surviving family members blame the primary caregiver—the one child who cared for an ailing parent night and day, sacrificing personal priorities to keep the parent safe and comfortable—for the parent's death. I've seen respectable, well-to-do offspring descend on the family home just hours after the death of a parent to snatch up an old photo or a sentimental heirloom before the other family members could get to it. It's a mistake to take these actions at face value and intervene with an appeal to fairness. Instead, they're the distorted outworking of fear, guilt, and anxiety over a loss that just doesn't make sense, a loss that hangs over life from now on like a black cloud. A rabbi or pastor has to recognize and honor that profound sense of loss, even if we can't approve of all the behavior it might produce.

But sometimes the death of a patriarch brings the opposite response, peace among the survivors.

> This is how long Avraham lived: 175 years. Then Avraham breathed his last, dying at a ripe old age, an old man full of years; and he was gathered to his people. Yitz'chak and Yishma'el his sons buried him in the cave of Makhpelah, in the field of 'Efron the son of Tzochar the Hitti, by Mamre. (25:7–9)

At Abraham's death, the estranged brothers Isaac and Ishmael come together again. The Narrator notes God's blessing on Isaac after Abraham's death, and then immediately goes on to list the generations of Ishmael, who fathers twelve sons, which become twelve tribes, paralleling the twelve tribes of Israel. Moreover, the Narrator describes Ishmael's death a little later with the term *vayigva*, "he breathed his last" or "he expired" (25:17), a term, according to Rashi, which is usually applied only to the righteous (like Abraham at 25:8). Somehow, upon the death of Abraham, not only are Isaac and Ishmael reunited, at least briefly, but Ishmael himself gains in stature.

We see the same pattern at the death of Isaac, as his two sons, the sibling-rival sons Esau and Jacob, join together to bury him. Of course, there had already been a dramatic reconciliation scene between the two earlier, when Esau ran to meet Jacob, threw his arms around his neck and kissed him, and they wept, and Esau graciously accepted Jacob's extravagant gift of flocks of goats and sheep, along with cattle, donkeys, and camels (33:4–11). But that scene ended with Jacob refusing Esau's offer to travel together, and the brothers going their separate ways (Gen. 33:12–18). Now, however, the brothers finally rejoin to bury their father.

> Yitz'chak lived to be 180 years old. Then he breathed his last [*vayigva*, the same term applied to Abraham and Ishmael earlier], died and was gathered to his people, an old man full of years; and his sons 'Esav and Ya'akov buried him. (35:28–29)

The Narrator here restores the original birth order—it's "Esau and Jacob" not "Jacob and Esau" who bury their father. Esau's disregard of the birthright and Jacob's scheming to obtain it are set aside at this final moment. In this scene it's not Jacob the chosen and Esau the rejected, but Esau and Jacob, older brother and younger brother, joined together to provide their father an honorable burial.

As with Ishmael after Abraham's death, the account immediately goes on to list the generations of Esau, which takes up an entire chapter (36) of Genesis. This list serves "a theological purpose."

> Esau was the subject of a divine oracle and the recipient of a patriarchal blessing (25:23; 27:39–40), and the data now given show how these were fulfilled in history. The rise and development of the Edomite tribes, like the fortunes of Israel, are determined by the workings of God's Providence and are part of His grand design of history.[13]

Esau is not Jacob, of course, and he will not bear the full legacy of Abraham and Isaac. But he is still a son, who receives blessing, including a homeland, and he is the ancestor of "the kings who reigned in the land of Edom before any king had reigned over the people of Isra'el" (36:31). Somehow, the death of Isaac brings all this to the fore, along with the revelation that the choice of one son does not require the rejection of the other. At the death of their fathers, Ishmael and Esau both receive confirmation of their blessing and their place in the divine narrative—a hint of God's boundless favor that lies deep below the surface of sibling rivalry. Ishmael and Esau seem to lose out in the rivalry, yet each one receives affirmation from the Lord. The story won't come to completion without them, as becomes evident at the death of their fathers. Let's see whether the same dynamic is at work in the death of Jacob.

The brothers are all present when Jacob "breathes his last"—*vayigva* again (49:33), and all are involved in his elaborate burial in the Promised Land. Then, after they return to Egypt, they regroup.

> Realizing that their father was dead, Yosef's brothers said, "Yosef may hate us now and pay us back in full for all the suffering we caused him." So they sent a message to Yosef which said, "Your father gave this order before he died: 'Say to Yosef, "I beg you now, please forgive your brothers' crime and wickedness in doing you harm."' So now, we beg of you, forgive the crime of the servants of the God of your father." Yosef wept when they spoke to him. (50:15–17)

Realizing (or literally "seeing") their father was dead implies "when the reality of the situation struck them on their return to Egypt."[14] With Jacob gone, the brothers realize the real Joseph can now emerge, and they are terrified. They fear the kind of response to the death of the patriarch that I described above, where family members turn on each other out of the pain and anxiety of their loss. The brothers might also fear that Joseph had kept the peace with them only to spare Jacob any additional sorrow—exactly as they had *failed* to spare Jacob sorrow when they sold Joseph into bondage. Now that Jacob is dead, this limit on Joseph's behavior is gone, and who knows what he will do? They instinctively might fear the kind of response Joanne experienced from her brother and sisters, although the roles are reversed here. Joseph is the solitary brother, who probably provided the most care for Jacob in his final years. But the brothers weren't being unrealistic in fearing he might turn on them. They're so fearful, in fact, that they send messengers to Joseph instead of appearing themselves. Joseph's reaction, according to the Midrash, is to exclaim, "My brethren thus suspect me!" (*Genesis Rabbah* 100:9). When Joseph realizes his brothers don't trust him, he's stung by their distrust, and he weeps. But when the brothers hear of his emotional response, they finally come in person.

> And his brothers too came, prostrated themselves before him and said, "Here, we are your slaves." But Yosef said to them, "Don't be afraid! Am I in the place of God? You meant to do me harm, but God meant it for good—so that it would come about as it is today, with many people's lives being saved. So don't be afraid—I will provide for you and your little ones." In this way he comforted them, speaking kindly to them. (50:18–21)

The brothers "prostrated themselves," literally falling down before Joseph, which is even more dramatic than their previous times of bowing down to him. They've begged Joseph to forgive them for their crimes (50:17), and now they describe themselves as his slaves . . . and act like it. But Joseph's words of comfort to his brothers make it clear he does indeed forgive them. He had probably forgiven them long before, even though he didn't use that word, when he first revealed himself to them and told them not to grieve or be angry at themselves for what they had done (45:4–8). Rabbi Sacks says this earlier incident is the first instance of human-to-human forgiveness pictured in the Tanakh. Even more, he writes, "This is *the first recorded moment in history in which one human being forgives another.*"[15]

Joseph's forgiveness of his brothers really is momentous. Human-to-human forgiveness frees us from the cruel, never-ending process of trying to pay for our misdeeds and getting others to pay for theirs—or resenting them if they don't. Forgiveness allows family life and community life to continue on, despite our inevitable shortcomings and even outright sins. Without forgiveness, as Joseph realized, we're stuck with distrust, which leads to compulsive control. If you are guilty and not forgiven for the past, I can't trust you to do the right thing in the future. And if I can't trust you, I have to control you and your behavior. Families without an adequate practice of forgiveness become arenas of domination and control, and of dogged resistance to control. Of course, forgiveness doesn't magically fix everything. If we have done wrong, we still have to make amends, and face the consequences of our actions. If we've been wronged, we still have to learn to relinquish control and begin to trust again. But forgiveness paves the way for this whole process of restoration, however extended it might be.

I agree with Rabbi Sacks that Joseph had likely forgiven his brothers years before Jacob's death. In fact, I believe he forgave them even before he revealed himself to them. Rabbi Sacks also reads it this way: "Joseph forgives his brothers without their asking for it, without their apology, and long before he tells them who he is."[16] But only after Judah demonstrates repentance by

offering his own freedom in exchange for Benjamin's can Joseph
begin to *show* his forgiveness. It's notable, though, that even at
that dramatic turning-point in the story, the brothers didn't ask
for forgiveness, but "maintained an unbroken silence."[17]

> Joseph's deeds and words (from chap. 45) had shown he
> wanted to be reconciled to his brothers, but they had
> never asked for forgiveness, so their feelings of guilt had
> continued to haunt them. Now with their father dead and
> the great funeral over, they are gripped by fear that all
> Joseph has done was motivated by affection for Jacob,
> not out of real love for them.[18]

Only now, in chapter 50, does the terminology of forgiveness
become explicit, as the brothers plead with Joseph: "Your father
gave this order before he died: 'Say to Yosef, "I beg you now,
please *forgive* your brothers' crime and wickedness in doing you
harm."'" So now, we beg of you, *forgive* the crime of the servants
of the God of your father" (50:16b–17, emphasis added).

The Tanakh normally portrays forgiveness as something
done by God, not by humans. The first discussion of forgiveness
in Genesis is the negotiation between Abraham and God over
Sodom. Abraham says:

> Maybe there are fifty righteous people in the city; will
> you actually sweep the place away, and not *forgive* it
> [same root as in 50:17] for the sake of the fifty righteous
> who are there? Far be it from you to do such a thing — to
> kill the righteous along with the wicked, so that the
> righteous and the wicked are treated alike! Far be it from
> you! Shouldn't the judge of all the earth do what is just?"
> *ADONAI* said, "If I find in S'dom fifty who are righteous,
> then I will *forgive* [same root again] the whole place for
> their sake." (18:24–26, emphasis added)

Only God can forgive in the absolute sense, dealing with all the sins of a person or a group. This is why some of the onlookers had a problem when Yeshua said to a paralyzed man, "Friend, your sins are forgiven you." This statement got the Torah-teachers and the Pharisees thinking, "Who is this fellow that speaks such blasphemies? Who can forgive sin except God?" (Luke 5:20–21). It's a reasonable question, because we humans can't forgive sin in any kind of general or final sense. But when one person sins against another, the victim of that sin can forgive—as first demonstrated by Joseph.

Without forgiveness, the whole story of Joseph and his brothers never could have reached this final chapter. That's why I believe Joseph forgave even earlier, even before he revealed himself. I believe he had to forgive before he could be willing to let them prove themselves. In the last chapter, we looked at the process of restoring trust, but forgiveness precedes restoration of trust. The offender has to earn my trust, which doesn't happen immediately, and forgiveness provides him the opportunity to do so. In other words, forgiveness in itself doesn't restore the relationship, but it makes room for restoration. When Joseph responds to his brothers' request for forgiveness in Genesis 50, he speaks as one who had long since forgiven them, and who had provided a way for them to regain his trust.

## Joseph restored

In earlier chapters we considered the tale of the hero's journey and how it sheds light on the story of Joseph and his brothers (and vice-versa). Often the hero sustains a deep wound on his journey, sometimes a lifelong wound that is never fully healed. We saw how *The Lord of the Rings* builds on the hero's journey theme. In that story, Frodo Baggins, early in his journey,

is wounded by a Black Rider, who attacks him and leaves the tip
of his dagger in Frodo's shoulder before he's driven off. Even
after Frodo succeeds in his mission and turns toward home, the
wound remains.

> 'Are you in pain, Frodo?' said Gandalf quietly as he rode
> by Frodo's side.
>
> 'Well, yes, I am,' said Frodo. 'It is my shoulder. The
> wound aches, and the memory of darkness is heavy on
> me. It was a year ago today.'
>
> 'Alas! there are some wounds that cannot be wholly
> cured,' said Gandalf.[19]

Jacob, in his hero's journey, is wounded by the "man" at Peniel,
who touches his hip socket, so that his hip is put out of joint. "As
the sun rose upon him he went on past P'ni-El, limping at the
hip. This is why, to this day, the people of Isra'el do not eat the
thigh muscle that passes along the hip socket—because the man
struck Ya'akov's hip at its socket" (32:32–33). Jacob's wound is
not mentioned again, but it would seem to be a permanent
affliction. His descendants permanently remember it by
abstaining from eating the thigh muscle of the hip socket. This
abstention remains part of the kosher laws to this day, a reminder
of the wounding of the hero.

If all this is the case, we might ask how Joseph is wounded.
His wounds weren't physical, and couldn't be seen, but they
were there—the wounds of betrayal at the hands of his own
brothers. It's often said that emotional wounds can be as painful
and as debilitating as physical wounds, or even more so. Joseph
is emotionally wounded by the very ones who should have
understood and protected him. His lengthy testing of his brothers
years later strikes some readers as manipulative and even

vengeful. But he's not trying to get even; he's trying to get *healed*. He needs evidence his brothers have changed, so that he can not only forgive, but also begin to trust them again. Judah provided the evidence Joseph sought when he offered himself in exchange for Benjamin, Joseph's stand-in (44:33–34). Judah demonstrated deep repentance for being party to the betrayal of Joseph, and thus opened the way for restoration.

When Judah offered himself, then, he brought healing not only to the fragmented family, but also to the deep wounds of Joseph's soul. *The Lord of the Rings* records an ancient saying, "The hands of the king are the hands of a healer." [20] Judah is head of the kingly tribe, and he brought healing through offering himself. Now, years later, Jacob's death isn't going to reopen Joseph's old wounds, because they are healed. And Joseph, the one who is healed, brings healing to his family through forgiveness.

The scene of forgiveness in Genesis 50, coming as it does at the culmination of the whole story, teaches us four vital lessons.

1. **Forgiveness must be explicit.** Joseph comforted his brothers when he revealed himself to them, and he watched out for them for years in Egypt. Yet the word "forgive" had not been spoken, as far as the text itself tells us, until now. Sometimes in counseling couples, when the offending party apologizes and admits his (or her) wrongdoing, I'll have him say, "Please forgive me." If the offended party is willing to forgive, I'll ask her to say, "I forgive you." These words, like "I love you," need to be said aloud. And sometimes they need to be reiterated. We can't be like the one husband who told his wife, "I said 'I love you' when I proposed, and if anything changes, I'll let you know." Likewise with "I forgive you." We can't just say it once and expect it to last a

lifetime. A caveat here, though: It's hard to overdo "I love you," but you can definitely overdo "I forgive you." Overdoing it can make the offender feel like you're rubbing his face in his offense rather than letting it go. You may need to repeat "I forgive (or I forgave) you" a few times over the years, but not every day.

2. **Forgiveness needs to be renewed.** It may need to be applied to new conditions. The death of Jacob changes the whole family system, and without explicit forgiveness the family members won't be able to adjust to it. Also, Joseph and his brothers are getting older by the time Jacob dies, and forgiveness becomes even more important, because they know unforgiveness can become part of the inherited narrative for coming generations. It can be handed down from one generation to the next and become a bitter part of the family legacy. The legacy of Jacob's family had been rooted in sibling rivalry. Jacob had a fierce rivalry with Esau that only began to be resolved after both had become fathers. Jacob's own family was built upon the rivalry of his two sister-wives Leah and Rachel, and that rivalry continued on among their sons. Joseph's forgiveness has the power to break this dynamic, but it needs to be restated specifically as a new generation is ready to come more fully on the scene.

3. **Forgiveness reframes the past.** Joseph tells his brothers, "You meant to do me harm, but God meant it for good." This realization is not the basis for his forgiveness; he doesn't forgive *because* God did something good with the brothers' sin. If that were the case, we wouldn't be able to forgive—or we have an excuse not to forgive—the sins that have no apparent good result. It's because Joseph forgives that he's able to *see* that God used the brothers' sin for good. He tells

his brothers this, not as a condition for forgiveness, but to enable them to receive his forgiveness despite their guilt and shame. Joseph's statement "shows the power of a religious vision to *reframe* history, liberating ourselves from the otherwise violent dynamic of revenge and retaliation. . . . It includes the freedom to *reshape* our understanding of the past, *healing* some of the legacy of its pain."[21]

4. **Forgiveness makes trust possible.** Forgiveness does not equal restored trust, but it allows the offender to earn trust anew. This is why I believe Joseph had already forgiven his brothers before he put them through the elaborate test in Genesis 42-44 to determine whether he could ever trust them again.

When we practice forgiveness, we discover new meaning to our past, including our past sufferings. We are no longer victims who are just trying to survive the things that happen to us. Rather, by forgiving, we "become a *hero* instead of a victim in the story [we] tell."[22] By forgiving, we reframe our history of offense or abuse or betrayal into a hero's journey.

First, forgiving empowers us to discover meaning and value in what before had been only a sad tale of loss. This reframing of the past transforms the future. It allows the future to be about hope and possibility instead of revenge, domination or victimization.

Second, by forgiving, we take charge of the story and ultimately hand over charge of our story to God. It's no longer just an event or string of events that happened to us, but an event we can build upon for good. Becoming a hero instead of a victim in the story we tell doesn't mean we claim extraordinary powers, or excuse what was done to us. Rather, it means we seize the initiative in defining the meaning of what was done to us. We shape our own story, in partnership with God, including its future installments. Thus, after the climax of forgiveness, Joseph can provide direction for his future, and the book of Genesis can end on a note of hope.

## Freed for a Future

When the brothers prostrate themselves before Joseph, Judah of course is among them—the same Judah to whom Jacob had said, "Your father's sons will bow down *before you*" (49:8, emphasis added). Joseph might appear to win in this contest of dominance, as he receives the last bow. The story doesn't end with that scene, however, but with a final death scene:

> Yosef said to his brothers, "I am dying. But God will surely remember you and bring you up out of this land to the land which he swore to Avraham, Yitz'chak and Ya'akov." Then Yosef took an oath from the sons of Isra'el: "God will surely remember you, and you are to carry my bones up from here." So Yosef died at the age of 110, and they embalmed him and put him in a coffin in Egypt. (50:24–26)

Just as Jacob had done, Joseph in his final moments looks to the future of his beloved family, the tribes of Israel, before making arrangements for his own future. He has left behind the old rivalry with his brothers to imagine an abundant future for them all, and to point the way for us. Joseph, like Jacob before him, demonstrates a personal faith that's not primarily about his own well-being or eternal destiny, but about God's eternal purposes, and how they will play out on the earthly stage.

There's something else going on in these final instructions that we can easily miss. Joseph, the dominant one, the one before whom all the brothers, including Judah, have bowed down several times, becomes dependent on his brothers in the end. And he unabashedly states his dependence: "God will surely remember you, and you are to carry my bones up from here." Here is a divine reversal.[23] Joseph the leading son who saves his entire family, Joseph the ruler of Egypt who is embalmed like an Egyptian and placed in an Egyptian coffin, turns his gaze from Egypt to the land promised to his forefathers—and must depend on his brothers to get him there.

In Jewish tradition, care for the deceased is regarded as one of the highest levels of ethical behavior, precisely because the deceased cannot care for themselves, and can't pay us back. Back at the beginning of our parasha, Jacob had called for Joseph and said to him,

> "Please, if I have found favor in your eyes, please place your hand under my thigh and deal with me in kindness and truth. Please do not bury me in Egypt! I will lie down with my fathers and you shall carry me out of Egypt and bury me in their grave." (Gen. 47:29b–30, my translation)

The phrase "kindness and truth" is *chesed v'emet* in Hebrew. The Midrash comments, "The love [*chesed*] shewn to me after death is true [*emet*]. A man sometimes honours his father through fear or shame, but this love after death is a true love" (*Genesis Rabbah* 96). The kindness people do for the dead is called *chesed shel emet*, kindness of truth, or genuine kindness, because the dead cannot reciprocate.[24] Joseph, his brothers' provider and savior, places himself in their care, and asks them to help when he becomes helpless, when he can never pay them back. He can't get himself back to the homeland, and so he becomes dependent on his brothers to carry him there.

In this final scene, Joseph recalibrates the triangulation he described when he told his brothers, "You meant to do me harm, but God meant it for good." In that triangulation, God stands between the brothers and Joseph, transforming their harmful intent into good. In that triangulation, Joseph has the direct connection to God, and the brothers receive God's benefit through him. Now, Joseph resets the triangle. God himself will remember the brothers directly, not through Joseph's mediation, and the brothers will be the instruments of benefit to Joseph, rescuing his bones from Egypt to bear them up to the land of promise (50:24–25). Joseph has been the favored son, but now the brothers will receive God's favor as well—boundless favor.

Joseph's final instructions differ from Jacob's final instructions in an important way. Jacob had told Joseph, "I will lie down with my fathers and you shall carry me out of Egypt and bury me in their grave." After his final blessing on the twelve sons, Jacob reiterated this instruction to all of them: "I am to be gathered to my people. Bury me with my ancestors in the cave that is in the field of 'Efron the Hitti, the cave in the field of Makhpelah, by Mamre, in the land of Kena'an" (49:29–30). The brothers carried out this wish promptly; after a period of mourning in Egypt, they transported Jacob to Canaan for burial. Joseph, in contrast, provides for an intermediate period. It's not until God brings all the children of Israel up from Egypt that Joseph's bones are to go up with them for his final burial. Why the delay? Sarna comments on Joseph's words, *God will surely remember you*—"This reassuring profession of faith, made fifty-four years after Jacob's death, betrays a serious deterioration in the situation of the Israelites in Egypt in the intervening period." Sarna then addresses our question: "Why Joseph does not request immediate interment in the land of his fathers is not explained; no doubt, he knows that present conditions are unfavorable."[25]

In addition to this practical need for delay because of unfavorable conditions, however, there's also a deeper reason.

Joseph, who was rejected and then separated from his brothers for over twenty years, will not allow himself to be separated again. For as long as his brothers remain in Egypt, he too will remain with them. There will come a time when the entire family of Abraham will be reunited in the Promised Land. Until that time, however, Joseph foregoes the privilege of being buried with his fathers. Until the brothers are able to go home, Joseph will not go home. He will remain with his brothers, and when they do depart, he will depend upon his brothers to bear him up and carry him to his resting place.

And so the tale comes full-circle. It began as the brothers cast Joseph into a pit and returned home without him. Now, at the end, Joseph will descend into another pit, death itself, confident that his brothers will lift him up and carry him with them when they take their journey home.[26] "So Yosef died at the age of 110, and they embalmed him and put him in a coffin in Egypt." Joseph dies with his mission fulfilled and his family restored at last.

# Conclusion

# Living a life of favor

One of my all-time favorite books opens with a warning:

NOTICE

PERSONS attempting to find a motive in this narrative will be prosecuted; persons attempting to find a moral in it will be banished; persons attempting to find a plot in it will be shot.

BY ORDER OF THE AUTHOR,
Per G.G., Chief of Ordnance.

The author is Mark Twain, and he wants us to let Huck Finn's story just be a story. Don't reduce it to a morality play or an allegory, or—contra the temptation that's particularly great with Bible stories—to a mine for hidden doctrinal propositions. Let the story live and breathe within its own ambiguities, mysteries and depths. On the other hand, if we really enter into a great story, we won't leave unchanged. We will learn from it—not reducing it to a series of proof texts of what we already knew, but allowing the story to challenge and expand what we thought we already knew to reveal new insights.

With a glance back at Mark Twain, then, I didn't set out to write a self-help book based on the story of Joseph and his brothers. I've attempted to let their story be, above all, a story.

The power of a story is that it can teach profound truths without overly simplifying things, without lecturing us or moralizing. A great story opens up new possibilities of thought and action. So, as we've listened deeply to this story, I hope we've come to see some new things that might have practical, even self-help implications. Perhaps we've gained some new insight into our inner selves, our friendships and families, and even God himself. The sages of Midrash listened deeply to the stories of Abraham, Isaac, and Jacob and didn't hesitate to explore (the literal meaning of *midrash*) the implications for the lives of their descendants. So let's do likewise.

## Favor and God

The story reveals that our forefathers all experienced God's favor. They all practiced favor themselves, sometimes wisely and sometimes not, but always as an inseparable part of who they were as fathers. Their practice of fatherhood reflected the fatherhood of God, who had favored and chosen them. In the Bible, God reveals himself to the world, and acts within the world, through a favored family, which becomes a favored nation, which brings forth a favored son who has universal redemptive impact. As we embrace favor as an aspect of fatherhood, especially God's, we discover its redemptive benefit to all. So without overanalyzing the tale, or reducing it to a collection of theological verities, let's consider three discoveries about how favor relates to God himself.

### Understanding favor helps us understand God as a father.

The stories of Genesis center on both on the human dimension of being favored, and even more, the divine dimension of choosing to favor. The God we read about in Genesis, and throughout the rest of Scripture, is a God who chooses. Early in the biblical narrative, he favors Abel and his offering over Cain and his offering, and he continues to make choices like that. Sometimes his choice seems in response to a person's merit. In the days before the flood, for example, God was thinking about sending judgment upon the whole human race, "But Noach found grace in the sight of *Adonai*" (Gen. 6:8). At first it sounds like God just chose this one man out of the blue to receive his mercy, but the next verse tells us: "Here is the history of Noach. In his generation, Noach was a man righteous and wholehearted; Noach walked with God" (Gen. 6:9). Apparently Noah *deserved* the grace he found in God's sight. But later on, God favored Jacob over Esau before they were even born, telling their mother, Rebekah, "The older will serve the younger" (Gen. 25:23), "so that God's plan might remain a matter of his sovereign choice, not dependent on what they did, but on God, who does the calling" (Rom. 9:11).

This whole idea of undeserved favor is scandalous in today's world, but as we've seen, it's essential to understanding God. "The scriptural doctrine of divine capacity for choice demonstrates that purpose and personality, not blind mechanism, are at the heart of the universe."[1] This applies not just to understanding God generally, but especially as a father. We have to recognize "that to substitute an impartial judge for a loving father would eliminate the preference for the specially favored but would also deprive all of them of a father."[2]

So we come to a paradox. If we want to believe in a God who can love us, who can be a father concerned about each of his children in particular, we have to accept his capacity to favor, or not favor, according to his own will and purposes, and not our own—or those of any theological system we might construct.

In the same way, God may favor different children in different ways, according to their unique qualities. My mother, of blessed memory, used to collect Jewish figurines by folk artist David Kaplan. Before moving out of her own home, she gave one figurine each to me and my two brothers. My oldest brother, a successful entrepreneur, got a figurine of a man peddling his wares at the street market. My next brother, a skilled contractor, received one of a man at a sewing machine—a skilled tailor plying his trade. My mother gave me a figurine of a rabbinic-looking man, pondering an open book at his desk—just as I love to do. My mother favored us all (and had been searching for a figurine for my sister as well), but recognized our differences. She was a real, live, flesh-and-blood mother who loved all her children, but related to them in different ways according to their different personalities. To insist on a featureless, level playing-field of parental love would have deprived my siblings and me of the unique warmth my mother wanted to express to each of us individually.

Likewise, to expect God to treat everyone identically would rob him of personality, and turn our sense of his love into an abstraction that might sound nice but wouldn't do us much good emotionally or spiritually. As we recognize this, we also recognize that God's favor toward different children is not only different, but sometimes qualitatively so. God favors the children of Israel in a way he does not favor any other nation—which leads to our next point.

**Those who honor God will honor his choice of favor.**

God's "capacity for choice" is essential to his fatherhood. A non-choosing God is foreign to the picture of deity painted by Scripture, but we humans have not entirely made our peace with this whole concept. If we have to accept a God who shows favor, we want it to be a God who favors *us*. The stories of Genesis show how this desire for favor becomes a desire not just for favor, but at the expense of everyone else. In this zero-sum drama, if I'm not the favored one, I'll reject the one who is. But if I do that, Joseph's story warns, I'm actually rejecting the father who made the choice of one to favor.

This zero-sum understanding of favor has damaged the relationship between Judaism and Christianity almost from the outset. Let's explore this contested relationship for a moment. It's an important topic in its own right, and it has important implications for our understanding of favor.

A few years ago, one Middle Eastern archbishop declared, "We Christians cannot speak of the 'promised land' as an exclusive right for a privileged Jewish people. There is no longer a chosen people—all men and women of all countries have become the chosen people."[3] The archbishop was taking aim at the modern state of Israel, but he was also reflecting traditional Christian supersessionism, or replacement theology, which sees God's election of Israel as *superseded* by the election of the church.[4] This archbishop is hardly unique, or even in the minority; on the contrary, he represents a dominant position within the church, though he may be expressing it more bluntly than most. In this view, favor, or election, is a zero-sum matter, in which the election of one requires the rejection of the other.

This belief is based on some passages within the New Testament and sustained by ignoring other ones. Thus, for example, Peter applies the same terminology God uses to describe Israel's unique calling to the new Messiah-believing community: "But you are a chosen race, a royal priesthood, a holy nation, a people for his own possession, that you may proclaim the excellencies of him who called you out of darkness into his marvelous light" (1 Peter 2:9, ESV). Since Peter applies the old biblical description of Israel to the new Yeshua-following community, you could conclude this new community has replaced Israel. Paul, on the other hand, insists Israel's unique election stands:

> As regards the gospel, they are enemies for your sake. But as regards election, they are beloved for the sake of their forefathers. For the gifts and the calling of God are irrevocable. (Rom. 11:28–29, ESV)

We could multiply such examples on both sides of the question. Clearly the New Testament sometimes applies the language of election, derived from the Tanakh, to the new community of Yeshua-followers, yet the New Testament also supports the continuing election of Israel, the literal descendants of Abraham, Isaac and Jacob, as portrayed throughout the Tanakh. This both/and approach reflects the narrative mode of Scripture, with all its subtleties and nuance, but the cold logic of Western thought insists the election of one means the rejection of the other. The New Testament sustains the notion of elect Israel, elect even in its current (and partial) alienation from Messiah Yeshua, alongside an elect assembly in Messiah drawn from all nations. It's both/and. Christianity theology, and often Christian behavior as well, has had a hard time embracing this view, instead contesting Israel's continuing election.

Michael Wyschogrod ties this contest over election to the story of Joseph and his brothers.

> Just as Joseph's brothers rebelled against the favor shown by their father toward this one child of his, so the nations refuse to accept the election of Israel. . . . Just as Joseph suffered for his deeds, so has Israel; just as Joseph retained the election, proving worthy of it, so has Israel.[5]

The mystery the church has often failed to comprehend is that its election in no way diminishes Israel's. Indeed, the election of the church *depends upon* the election of Israel, as God said to Abraham, "In your seed all the nations of the earth will be blessed" (Genesis 22:18, TLV). The chosen seed of the chosen people, the family of Abraham, will be the source of blessing for all peoples. God's favor of the one benefits the many.

The brothers can never replace Joseph as their father's favorite, but once they accept his favored position—or more to the point, once they embrace and support Jacob's choice to favor Joseph—they are able to benefit from it. This is a key to reversing supersessionism or replacement theology. Jewish-Christian reconciliation demands a repudiation of replacement theology, and an affirmation of God's continuing covenant with Israel, "for the gifts and the calling of God are irrevocable" (Rom. 11:29).

As we've seen, Jacob's final prophetic word over all his sons expresses unique favor for not just one, but two of his sons, Judah and Joseph. This points beyond the zero-sum, either/or understanding of favor that's somehow lodged in the human psyche, has shaped Jewish-Christian relations from the beginning. In our day we're seeing a transformation of that relationship through a deep reconciliation between Jews and Christians, the church and the synagogue.

The Messianic Jewish community, of which I'm a member, is a sign of that reconciliation. Because Israel is not replaced, Jews who accept Yeshua as Messiah need not switch religions or communal identification. We remain Jewish in outlook, practice and identity, as we seek to follow Yeshua. Even in our community, however, there's much confusion over the issue of favor. Some of our Jewish members feel their Jewish identity should now be diminished or shelved in favor of a new "messianic" identity. Some of our Gentile members feel it would be better if they were Jewish, or that they really are Jewish now that they're part of a Messianic Jewish community. Here's the model we should instead promote in our community: Jews as Jews, fully engaged members of the chosen people, and Gentiles as Gentiles, individuals chosen out of the non-chosen nations, maintaining their unique identities as they serve Messiah Yeshua together. This model is a living answer to the error of replacement theology.

I've focused on the relationship between Christians and Jews because it so powerfully demonstrates that those who claim to love the Father must affirm and support the one he has chosen. This idea works in our families and congregations as well. Instead of getting drawn into a competition for favor, we can recognize and honor God as Father, a father who loves all his children equally but differently. God's favor toward Israel leads to great blessing for all nations.

> Because [God] said, "I will bless those who bless you, and curse him that curses you; in you shall all the families of the earth be blessed" (Gen. 12:3), he has tied his saving and redemptive concern for the welfare of all humankind to his love for the people of Israel. Only those who love the people of Israel can love the God of Israel. Israel is thus God's first-born, most precious in his eyes.[6]

In the same way, God's favor toward specific individuals, even within our family or congregation, leads to blessing for all, if we understand it properly.

**Favor accepted and affirmed benefits all.**

When Yeshua of Nazareth was ready to begin his service to the house of Israel, he went down to the Jordan River to be immersed by Yochanan. And then,

Immediately upon coming up out of the water, he saw heaven torn open and the Spirit descending upon him like a dove; then a voice came from heaven, "You are my Son, whom I love; I am well pleased with you." (Mark 1:10–11)

Here is an expression of boundless favor—a voice from heaven declaring Yeshua as the designated son, beloved of the father, and well pleasing to him. The father here, of course, is the God of Israel, whose words here echo his words to Abraham many centuries before: "Take your son, your only son, whom you love, Yitz'chak . . ." (Gen. 22:2). As Abraham was directed to offer up his beloved Isaac as a sacrifice, so the Father will offer up his beloved son, Yeshua, and his son will offer himself, as a sacrifice on behalf of all humankind.

The God of Israel is a God of mercy and compassion. When Moses pleaded with God, "I beg you to show me your glory!", God replied, "I will cause all my goodness to pass before you, and in your presence I will pronounce the name of *ADONAI*. Moreover, *I show favor to whomever I will*, and I display mercy to whomever I will. But my face you cannot see, because a human being cannot look at me and remain alive" (Ex. 33:18–20, emphasis added). Instead of revealing himself visibly, God spoke his name, describing his essence, to Moses:

*ADONAI* passed before him and proclaimed: "*YUD-HEH-VAV-HEH*!!! *Yud-Heh-Vav-Heh* [*ADONAI*] is God, merciful and compassionate, slow to anger, rich in grace and truth; showing grace to the thousandth generation, forgiving offenses, crimes and sins; yet not exonerating the guilty. (Ex. 34:6–7)

Jewish tradition has identified thirteen attributes of God within this self-description, which it calls the Thirteen Attributes of Mercy.[7] If God in his fullest self-disclosure in the Torah reveals himself to be primarily about compassion and kindness, we can expect his favored one to be all about compassion and kindness as well. We can expect him to express his favored status in a way that benefits others, and this is exactly what we see in the life of Yeshua of Nazareth. As he sums it up, "For the Son of Man did not come to be served, but to serve—and to give his life as a ransom for many" (Mark 10:45). God's favor so boundlessly poured out on Yeshua becomes a source of benefit to all.

This understanding of God changes the way we view favor. The journey of the favored hero ends in benefit and redemption for those around him. We're not to fight over the gift of favor, but to receive the blessing of the favored one who is among us.

**The remedy for favoritism.**

Joseph's story opens with his father clearly favoring him above his brothers, and even showing favoritism. In current thinking, the solution to such favoritism is equality and inclusion. Scripture on the other hand, especially in Joseph's story, has a completely different remedy: accepting the chosenness of the chosen, honoring God by supporting his choice, and finding one's own identity within the context that choice creates. Jacob isn't wrong to favor Joseph, as the story reveals in the end. He's probably wrong to express his favor through his insensitive display of favoritism, but the remedy for Jacob's favoritism isn't absolute equality, and it certainly isn't getting rid of the chosen one; it's accepting the father's desire. Likewise, the biblical issue of election isn't going to be resolved in today's world by defying or ignoring it, but by affirming God's choice.

This principle applies to God's choice of Israel, and it also applies to relationships within our own families and communities. We don't live in a leveled-out, totally egalitarian world, but we do live with a God who provides boundless favor through his favored one, Messiah Yeshua. The favored one lives a life of sacrificial service, so that God's special favor of the one becomes a source of blessing for the many.

Of course, even with this understanding of favor, it still isn't likely to be the most popular idea in our age of inclusion. The idea of chosenness is antithetical to today's sense of radical egalitarianism. "No one should be favored or chosen above anyone else, even if it benefits the non-chosen." In fact, the typical modern would say, it doesn't matter whether someone else wants to favor you or not. It's only what you think of yourself, what's right for you, that matters. But the Scriptures reveal that being chosen by another matters too—and far more. Favor is an inherent part of God's reality as Father, and properly understood, is a source of blessing to those who want to know him.

## Favor and identity

We are living today with an epidemic of anxiety and depression, particularly among younger people. The National Institute of Mental Health (NIMH) reports that in 2015:

- 16.1 million (est.) adults aged 18 or older in the United States had at least one major depressive episode in the past year. This number represented 6.7% of all U.S. adults.[8]

- 3 million (est.) adolescents aged 12 to 17 in the United States had at least one major depressive episode in the past year. This number represented 12.5% of the U.S. population aged 12 to 17.[9]

These numbers cover only major depressive episodes, and don't include less-severe forms of the condition, so the total number suffering from some form of depression in a given year is estimated to be about 10% of the population. But astounding as this number is, anxiety is even more prevalent than depression. In 2015, clinical anxiety—such as generalized anxiety disorder, post-traumatic stress disorder, various phobias, or obsessive-compulsive disorder—affected up to 18% of the adult population, with nearly a quarter of these individuals, or over 4% of our entire adult population, experiencing "severe" anxiety. Numbers were similar or even higher among youth.[10] It's hard to escape the conclusion that we are in the midst of an epidemic of depression and anxiety. The story of Joseph and his brothers can help us respond to the epidemic, at least in our own lives and communities.

One factor behind widespread anxiety is the perfect-storm combination of seemingly limitless personal choices to make and a flimsy basis for making any choices at all. In the age of the selfie, our culture tells us we have endless options and can make whatever we like of life and ourselves. Even gender is no longer seen as something inborn, but as a sort of accessory to self that we can choose and customize. And the same culture tells us that all of our choices are subjective, that there are no solid parameters beyond ourselves to guide us. Very stressful!

At the close of 2016, the Barna Group published its annual survey of current trends, which included "The Morality of Self-Fulfillment," an attempt to fill the void left by the culture's rejection of traditional religious morality.

There is growing concern about the moral condition of the nation, even as many American adults admit they are uncertain about how to determine right from wrong, often opting to look within themselves rather than to any external, more-traditional sources of authority. Barna has dubbed this new moral code, "The Morality of Self-Fulfillment" in which Americans value "finding themselves" as the highest good.[11]

So, we have endless options, but how do we choose one over any other? The Morality of Self-Fulfillment tells us to look within to find out what's going to be fulfilling, what's going to make us happy. According to Barna, the vast majority of adults believe "[t]he best way to find yourself is by looking within yourself" (91% of US adults; 76% of "practicing Christians"), and "To be fulfilled in life you should pursue the things you desire most" (86% of US adults; 72% of "practicing Christians"). At the same time, rates of depression and anxiety keep on spiking.

Our extreme anxiety levels give evidence of a culture-wide identity crisis. We have to figure out for ourselves who we are, and we're not given any values or principles to guide us—other than self-fulfillment. In the midst of all this uncertainty, Joseph's journey might help us find our way. It's a bracing alternative to the Morality of Self-Fulfillment. I suppose you could argue that Joseph found fulfillment by pursuing what he desired most—but what he desired most in the end wasn't about himself (despite his selfie-esque beginnings). He desired the healing and restoration of his family, and reunion with his elderly father—very traditional values. Even more counter-culturally, Joseph found himself not by looking within, but by taking the long and arduous journey of identity formation.

A clear, viable identity is the remedy to our age of anxiety. Our religious traditions offer such an identity. The tradition says to a Jewish young person, "You're a Jew. You're part of an ancient people with an amazing history and stellar values. Find your identity there." Or it might say to a Christian kid, "You're a believer; you're born again. Find your identity in union with Christ." These identities line up with Scripture, but Scripture also shows the way identity is formed. It's not only through embracing a set of values or beliefs, as good as they might be, but through taking a journey. The heroes of Scripture discover who they are through the journey they endure.

This authentic identity gained on the journey contrasts with the accessorized identity offered by our dominant culture. Indeed, it offers so many options for accessorized identity that it fuels our anxiety and depression. The hero's journey is about identity formed through testing. The hero is poor, overlooked, unappreciated, and is going to save the whole tribe in the end. But to finally become a hero, he or she has to endure a difficult journey and overcome great trials. Joseph's mistake early in his story was to treat his identity as something he can just receive and put on—like an accessory. Favor is a free gift, and he can put on his noble tunic as a sign of favor, but his true identity as the one who saves the nations and all Israel is something he must acquire through the trials of exile and servitude. He can put on the garment of favor, but he can't put on his authentic identity. As we've seen, on the way to gaining this identity, Joseph puts on and takes off, or is stripped of, his garments several times.

Here's another paradox of favor: It sounds contradictory to speak of tested identity and of undeserved (and untested) favor in the same context. In the cold hallways of logic these two ideas are contradictory, but in the pathways of story they work together. The gift of favor provides confidence and strength for the journey ahead, in which authentic identity is formed through trials and adversity.

## Favor in life today

How do we embrace favor as a reality in our lives today? How do we learn to benefit from favor instead of yielding to the anxiety and gloom that surround us in today's culture? Heeding Mark Twain's warning, I won't reduce the magnificent tale of Joseph and his brothers to a how-to list. Still, it has some practical, 21st-century implications for us, if we hear it well.

### Eat the ice cream, don't measure it.

My wife, Jane, grew up with an older sister and a younger brother, all born within a year and a half of each other. Being so close in age brought opportunities for fun and shared experiences, but it also intensified the sibling rivalry that's always part of family life. Jane says the bickering and comparing once got so ridiculous that when it was time to serve a special family treat, their mother took out a block of ice cream, unwrapped it and measured off slices with a ruler so all the kids knew it was "fair."

Of course, the ice cream was a gift, and the point was to receive it and enjoy it—not measure it to make sure your gift was identical to your sibling's! Favor is a gift, and you don't have to compete to receive it. We can learn to take the time to savor what life has afforded us instead of grieving over what we don't get. It's Facebook wisdom, I guess, but it works: Why do we spend so much more energy complaining about the things we don't have than appreciating the things we *do* have?

In her book *Short Stories by Jesus*, the renowned New Testament scholar Amy-Jill Levine uncovers a similar point in Yeshua's parable of the Pharisee and the Tax Collector (Luke 18:9–14). In Levine's hyper-literal translation the story opens, "And he [Yeshua] even said to some of those believing in themselves that they are righteous and despising the rest this parable." Levine says the real issue here isn't so much "believing in ourselves that we are righteous" as it is "despising the rest"— that is, our zero-sum, comparison-based approach to God's favor. I'm righteous, you're not; I win, you lose. Levine doesn't believe the Pharisee's prayer is necessarily problematic, until he points the finger at "this tax collector" praying nearby.

Before we get to Levine's surprising conclusion, we should consider a point she makes about Christian readings of Yeshua's parable, including this one. She claims Christian interpreters repeatedly cast the Jews as the bad guys in these stories, with Christians as the good guys. So, in their reading of this particular parable,

> [T]he Pharisee—the one who in his own context would be seen as righteous and respected—is a negative figure wallowing in hypocritical sanctimoniousness. . . . The message of the parable then becomes that it is better to be a repentant tax collector than a sanctimonious Pharisee, and better to be a Christian saved by grace than a Jew who despises others and teaches salvation by works.[12]

In other words, this sort of interpretation brings us back into the world of replacement theology I described earlier, into the zero-sum idea that God's favor upon the body of Yeshua's followers must *replace* his favor upon the people of Israel, so that the church replaces Israel. From this view, it's a short step to the idea that Jews are by definition lost, hypocritical and far from God.

Levine counters this idea throughout her book, and with particular punchiness in this story. The parable concludes, "I tell you, this man went down to his home right with God rather than the other." But the Greek phrase translated "rather than the other" could just as plausibly read "alongside the other," according to Levine. She says the problem with the either/or interpretation of a saved tax-collector and a lost Pharisee is that "it prompts exactly the same type of dualistic, judgmental system that Jesus speaks against, for it suggests the response, 'Thank you, God, that I am not like that Pharisee.'" But she continues,

> Jesus and his fellow Jews were not bound in their thinking by the social-science insistence upon limited good; they knew that the God of Israel was generous. In their view, there is enough grace for Pharisee and tax collector both.[13]

Yeshua himself, Levine claims, taught boundless favor—enough grace for all. Don't measure the ice cream of favor; don't begrudge your brother or sister their portion; just enjoy your share. This leads to a second point.

**Get more favor by giving it away.**

So, if I don't have to compete to receive the gift of favor, how *do* I get it? Here's a final paradox: I gain favor, boundless favor, by *giving* boundless favor. In my family and friendships, and even in my own sense of self, if I feel I'm on the short end of favor, I need to *give* more favor to others.

For example, when counseling, I often need to remind married couples that fairness isn't the goal of marriage. In fact, seeking fairness, like the balanced distribution of chores or equal spending habits, is more often a snare than a boost to healthy marriage. Instead of trying to make sure a stay-at-home wife and mother is doing as much work as he is, the stressed-out husband should give her a freebie when he gets home. He can whisk her and the kids off to a fun and affordable dinner, or make dinner for all of them, without wondering how that balances on the time-clock. The roles can be reversed, of course, if both parents work outside the home, or if the husband is a stay-at-home dad. Another freebie is praise or affirmation. The critical wife can work on recognizing the good thing her husband did that day, even if it's only one thing, and affirm it, sincerely, simply, and with no strings attached. Let's say she feels he's generally unengaged, clueless and boring, but she did walk in on him having a fun, lively conversation with their four-year-old daughter. The wife can give him the freebie: "Honey, the way you were talking with Allison was so sweet. You really made her laugh." Period. Nothing about, "Why don't you do that more often?" or "Why can't you be more fun with me?" Just freely giving him some recognition and affirmation—favor, in other words. Giving favor like this increases the favor I receive.

But what if I don't feel like giving a freebie? Aha! Here's where a key to real change comes in. An easily overlooked passage in Exodus provides that key. Moses had just come down from Mount Sinai with the Torah, the instructions of the LORD. "Then he took the Scroll of the Covenant and read it in the hearing of the people, and they said: 'All that the LORD has spoken we will do and we will hear'" (Ex. 24:7, literal translation). The reader expects the people to say, "We will hear (listen to, understand—all nuances of the Hebrew *shama* in this verse) and we will do," because we think hearing and understanding precede doing. But sometimes, this phrase indicates, we have to do before we really hear and understand. Sometimes we have to do before we *want* to do. Acting from the heart is essential, but we can change the heart from the outside in, by changing our actions and behavior, whether we feel like it or not.

David was a client of mine, a middle-aged engineer who was suffering from depression. One of the things he was depressed about was his marriage of 27 years. The kids had all left home, and he and his wife had grown apart. Judi was a paralegal with a demanding job, who came home tired and stressed out from work every day. "She doesn't have anything left for me," David said. "She doesn't even seem to realize that I'm struggling with this depression and need some cheering up. Instead, she comes home, throws something together for dinner, and plops down in front of the TV." I encouraged David to take the initiative in doing some small but meaningful things to relieve her stress— like "throwing something together" for dinner himself for both of them—even when he didn't at all feel like it. In fact, doing this sort of thing would be most effective *when he didn't feel like it.* Giving Judi some attention and favor even when he was depressed and felt like she didn't deserve it would help lift his depression, and might even help his marriage.

This approach is especially important to a life of favor. We can shut down our zero-sum thinking about favor by giving favor away. We can bestow favor through doing acts of kindness or affirmation toward others, even before we feel like doing them. This idea leads to another idea we can embrace in the story of Joseph and his brothers.

**Strive for character, not status.**

Joseph had to take the hero's journey, which included a unique task only he could fulfill. But he could fulfill it only after he was transformed and lifted above his preoccupation with status and competition. In the hero's journey, this transformation is often supernatural, but it doesn't happen at the wave of a wand. It comes about through trials—rejection by family, exile from home, betrayal, captivity, even threat of death. And this journey, no matter how difficult, results in benefit and service to the hero's family and tribe, even the family or tribe that earlier rejected him. The hero is a favored one, but in the hero's journey, especially in the hero-journeys of Genesis, favor is not meant to be worn as a fancy garment of status, but as the coveralls of service. Favor isn't maintained by hoarding it, but by giving it away. The Morality of Self-Fulfillment is inherently selfish, even narcissistic. In it, self is never satisfied. But in serving others, we find fulfillment and gain an identity.

In the hero's journey, true identity must emerge through testing. Such an identity is called *character*, and we build it through how we behave, how we treat others, through the attitudes we foster and the ones we drop. Right actions build character—and character is our only true possession,[14] because it never loses its value, and no one can take it from us. Striving for character reframes life's inevitable disappointments and frustrations into opportunities to build up virtues and strengths no one can tear down. Striving for character overcomes the quest for self-fulfillment, which, we're discovering anew in the 21st century, leads to stress, anxiety, and depression.

How often have you heard a parent answer a question about their hopes and desires for their children by saying, "I just want them to be happy"? It's become a truism in our times, but it's really not the best answer. Happiness usually comes when we're working on something else, as a byproduct. And even if our children could figure out a way to be happy by seeking happiness directly, character is a far more worthy goal. Character means becoming a genuinely decent human being, someone who is concerned about others and not just self. Someone who doesn't reduce life to the metrics of wealth, possessions and personal accomplishments, but who is an influence for good in the world.

So if we want our children, or others whom we mentor, to be men and women of character, we'll need to articulate clear values beyond personal happiness and success. We can be unashamed of promoting values like generosity, respect for all people, and sacrificial service to others, even if they are not in the mainstream. We can take the opportunity to point out the relevance of values like these in the midst of everyday life. The *Shema* (Deut. 6:4–9)[15], a biblical declaration recited twice daily by observant Jews, includes this admonition:

> These words, which I am ordering you today, are to be on your heart; and you are to teach them carefully to your children. You are to talk about them when you sit at home, when you are traveling on the road, when you lie down and when you get up.

Religious conviction, in other words, isn't just a personal, private matter. Our dominant culture is okay with personal religion, or "spirituality" as it likes to call it. But religious conviction is a family matter, and a public matter. We don't need to preach at our kids, but we do need to impress upon them our deep convictions, and as this passage details, to relate them to the context of our daily lives. If today's epidemic of anxiety comes in part from the overabundance of options combined with insufficient basis for making any choices, affirming clear values like these can help reverse the epidemic.

Furthermore, give your kids and followers an opportunity, and a challenge, to *own* the values you are promoting. We've all seen young people with seemingly strong values yield to temptation, their resolve to do right melting away like the morning dew in the heat of the day. We've also seen religious leaders, who represent strong values, get caught up in behavior that's the opposite of everything they stand for. Perhaps the problem is that these folks don't really *own* the values they proclaim. You can't make it with values you've just borrowed or put on for the occasion. Character is made up of owned values—values we've received and then learned deeply through experience; values for which we've paid a price. This is why we can speak of character as a possession; it belongs to us in a most profound way.

Children, or those under our influence, need opportunities to take ownership of their values, which means opportunities to put them into practice, to possibly fail, to pay a price. Over-protection and over-programming won't get this done.

Be an example. Live your values. We need to share our beliefs and convictions with those coming after us, and we also need to pay the price our beliefs and convictions demand. I've heard a story more than once from the days when families still went to drive-in movies. Some drive-ins charged by the number of passengers in the car, so the parents kept one kid in the front seat and hid the rest on the back-seat floor, covered with a blanket. After they paid the lower admission fee and found a spot to park, the kids could crawl out from under the blanket and enjoy the movie for free. Today's example might be telling the ticket agent at the theater your petite little daughter is eleven, so she can get the under-twelve price, when she's really thirteen. The next day you might try to lecture the kids about honesty, and you can imagine how far *that* will get.

Providing a positive example is just as important as avoiding a negative one. Show your kids what character looks like. Jane and I recently went out for breakfast with our 13-year-old granddaughter on a blustery winter morning. As we drove up to the restaurant, we noticed a man who appeared to be homeless and cold standing near the entrance. Homeless people, we're told, sometimes feel like no one sees them, like they're invisible. Jane, who's usually more spontaneous than I am, decided it wasn't enough to give him some money for food, and invited to come into the restaurant and have breakfast—with us! He turned out to be a pleasant fellow, and it all went well. Our granddaughter saw compassion and generosity in action in a way she'll remember far better than all the verbal instructions she's received, important as they are.

♦

The story of Joseph and his brothers is really Jacob's story, so we'll conclude this chapter, and this book, with an incident from the life of Jacob. He discovered his identity, and confirmed his character, in a mysterious encounter not long before the story of Joseph began.

Jacob, of course, began his life in an environment of zero-sum favor. He became a master of competing for favor, and his whole story unfolds in a series of tension-filled rivalries. He wrestled with Esau in the womb to be born first. This failed, but Jacob was still hanging on to Esau's heel at the moment of birth. Later he drove a tough bargain with Esau to purchase his birthright, and then cooperated with his mother, Rebekah, to usurp the blessing of the firstborn. Esau was understandably outraged, and Jacob had to flee, but then he spent the next twenty years wrestling with Laban, his uncle / father-in-law / boss, just to get a fair deal.

Jacob is pictured alone on only two occasions. The first came when Jacob camped alone at "a certain place" on the way out of the Promised Land, in flight from Esau (Gen. 28:11). Twenty-plus years later, when he's returning to the Promised Land, and about to meet up again with the dreaded Esau, we read: "And Jacob was left alone." Only now is Jacob finally alone . . . but then he ends up wrestling again, with a "man" until the break of day (32:25 [32:24 in Christian Bibles]). Until now, Jacob's identity has always been formed in tension with another person; first with Esau and then with Laban. Now, when Jacob is finally alone, we might think he's about to find his identity by looking within, in accord with the Morality of Self-Fulfillment. But Jacob is left alone with the divine. His identity is no longer being formed through self-exploration or zero-sum contest and comparison with other human beings, but in a face-to-face encounter with God (at least that's how Jacob describes it at the end of chapter 32). Whatever his exact identity, the "man" of Jacob's encounter comes from a reality beyond our normal categories, and beyond the categories of status and strife in which we normally think we'll work out our identity. Jacob's encounter reveals that we find ourselves, not by competing with other selves, or looking within ourselves, but by looking *beyond* ourselves.

Jacob, who had long ago wrestled with Esau over the blessing, now demands a blessing from his new wrestling partner. The wrestler responds by giving Jacob a new name, *Israel*, "for you have striven with God and with man and have prevailed" (32:29), or as Rashi paraphrases, "It shall no longer be said that the blessings came to you through trickery [*aq'vah*, from the same root as his old name *Ya'aqov*] and deceit, but with nobility [related to *s-r* in *Israel*] and openness." The identity Jacob gains through this encounter with the transcendent is noble and open, in contrast with the identity of comparison gained by struggling with other people. In like manner, we become noble and open as we seek a God-based identity in place of the usual human competition for approval, status and power.

But Jacob emerges from this encounter with something else—a bum hip. The "man" touched him there when Jacob saw he couldn't prevail, and in the end he had to limp away from the fight. Apparently, the touch on his hip joint impaired Jacob's wrestling prowess. He got his blessing, all right, but he also got a serious limitation, perhaps to keep him from striding back into his old habit of comparison and competition.

The rivalry for favor and status is deeply ingrained in human nature. The first crime in Genesis is fratricide, the murder of a brother, over competition for these very things. We grow up comparing ourselves with others, competing for recognition, and sometimes continue doing so long after we're grown up. This story reveals an encounter with the transcendent that can free us from all that, and give us a new identity as a prince or princess with God, as an Israel. But there's a cautionary note too: That encounter might leave us limping, less able to rely on ourselves, and more dependent on God.

This will sound like a contradiction (but we're in story mode, where contradictions are allowed): We can't gain our identity by looking within ourselves, but Jacob gains his identity when he's all by himself. Sure, he wrestles with a divine being, but humanly speaking, he's still alone. And this is precisely the point. He finds meaning not by looking within, but through *engaging with the divine other*, the being that transcends him and all human categories. Now he's going to live in response to the undeniable reality of this unknowable other, as an heir to boundless favor.

The journey of self-discovery yields to the discovery of what's utterly beyond self. There Jacob finds a blessing that is not produced through comparison and competition—a blessing that can't come from within, but only from God. His wrestling with God ends his wrestling with other mortals, and leaves him free to travel on in the afterglow of the divine encounter, even though his own strength is impaired. Jacob, the favored one and the giver of favor, continues his journey as Israel, a prince with God.

# Endnotes

## Preface

[1]  As a rule, *Midrash* is capitalized when it refers to a specific body of literature, especially *Midrash Rabbah*, a collection of midrashic writings beginning with Genesis Rabbah compiled in the fifth to sixth centuries of the Common Era, but containing much earlier material (*Midrash Rabbah, Genesis Volume One*, translated by Rabbi Dr. H. Freedman [London, New York: The Soncino Press, 1983], xxvii). Midrash is not capitalized when it refers to the interpretive technique itself.

[2]  Mayer Schachter-Haham. *Compound of Hebrew in Thousand Stem Words* (Jerusalem: Kiryat Sefer, Ltd., 1982), 144-145.

[3]  https://www.chesterton.org/democracy-of-the-dead/, citing *Orthodoxy*, pub, 1908; accessed 1/4/16.

[4]  "Tanakh" is an acronym of the first letters of *Torah, Nevi'im* (Prophets) and *Ketuvim* (Holy Writings). Some people say the Christian term "Old Testament" implies that these writings are obsolete, or a mere introduction to a New Testament, which is unacceptable from a Jewish perspective, and not really consistent with these Scriptures themselves. For this reason, we'll speak of the New Testament as the Apostolic Writings.

## Introduction

[1]  Abraham is introduced in B'reisheet as Abram, but it's customary in Jewish writing to refer to him as Abraham throughout his story.

[2]  *The JPS Torah Commentary, Genesis.* Commentary by Nahum M. Sarna (Philadelphia: The Jewish Publication Society, 1989), 16–17.

[3]  Unless otherwise indicated, all Scripture references are from *Complete Jewish Bible (CJB)*, copyright © 1998 by David H. Stern. All rights reserved.

4    R. Laird Harris, Gleason L. Archer, Jr., and Bruce Waltke. *Theological Wordbook of the Old Testament, Vol. I* (Chicago: Moody, 1980), 109.

5    Rabbi Jonathan Sacks. *Not in God's Name: Confronting Religious Violence* (New York: Schocken Books, 2015), 90.

6    I thank my friend and colleague Dr. Jeffrey Feinberg for pointing out the distinction between "chosen" and "favored," and suggesting that "favor" is a better description of Jacob's treatment of Joseph.

7    Adele Berlin and Marc Zvi Brettler, eds. *The Jewish Study Bible* (New York: Oxford University Press, 2004), *ad loc.* Emphasis added.

8    Sacks. *Not in God's Name*, 90.

9    Salvador Minuchin. *Families & Family Therapy* (Cambridge: Harvard University Press, 1974) 47.

10   Joseph Campbell. *The Hero With a Thousand Faces.* 1st edition, Bollingen Foundation, 1949. 2nd edition, Princeton University Press. 3rd edition, New World Library, 2008.

11   J.R.R. Tolkien. *The Fellowship of the Ring* (New York: Ballantine Books, 1965) 95.

12   Everett Fox. *The Five Books of Moses: Genesis, Exodus, Leviticus, Numbers, Deuteronomy: A New Translation with Introductions, Commentary, and Notes* (New York: Schocken Books, 1995), 54.

13   Ibid., 128.

## Chapter One

1    See discussion of identity formation in the Introduction.

2    Will Herberg, cited in Joel S. Kaminsky. *Yet I Loved Jacob: Reclaiming the Biblical Concept of Election* (Nashville: Abingdon Press, 2007), 1.

3    Michael Wyschogrod. *The Body of Faith: God and the People Israel* (Northvale, NJ: Jason Aronson, 1996), 64-65.

4    Ibid., 65.

5    Readers often assume the brothers tear or slash Joseph's tunic. Goldberg, for example, in *Midrash for Beginners* (Northvale, NJ: Jason Aronson, 1996) writes, "The brothers slaughter a goat and dip Joseph's torn ornamented coat into its blood." But nowhere in the text does it say the tunic is torn. I owe this insight to a group I recently studied with at Beth Shalom Messianic Congregation in Corona, California.

6    The verb here in 37:33 is different from the one used in 37:29 and 37:34, but both verbs depict similar action, and both are absent in all descriptions of Joseph's tunic.

7    Goldberg, 14.

8    Minuchin, 102.

9    Peter L. Steinke. *Congregational Leadership in Anxious Times* (Lanham, MD: Rowman & Littlefield, 2006), 116.

[10]  Edwin H. Friedman. *Generation to Generation: Family Process in Church and Synagogue* (New York: The Guilford Press, 2011), 27.

[11]  Steinke, 19. In his book, Steinke refers to Friedman as his mentor (136).

[12]  This of course is a different Tamar than the half-sister of Amnon, who wears the *ketonet passim* she ends up tearing. It's significant, though, that both Tamars are linked to the story of Joseph, and to the meaning of garments in the Bible, as we shall see.

[13]  See the discussion in Gordon J. Wenham, *Word Biblical Commentary: Genesis 16–50* (Grand Rapids: Zondervan, 2000), 363–365.

[14]  *JPS Torah Commentary* on Gen. 38:18.

[15]  *Theological Wordbook*, 198.

[16]  Jeffrey Enoch Feinberg. *Walk Genesis!* (Baltimore: Lederer Books, 1998), 163, citing Tos. HaShalem, Tan. Yashan 8.

[17]  *The Koren Pirke Avot*, trans. Rabbi Lord Jonathan Sacks, commentary by Rabbi Marc D. Angel (Jerusalem: Koren Publishers, 2016), Avot 4:22, 110, citing Rabbi Jacob.

[18]  Leon R. Kass. *The Beginning of Wisdom: Reading Genesis* (New York: Free Press, 2003), 530.

[19]  Wenham, *Genesis 16–50*, 364.

[20]  All examples taken from my counseling or rabbinic practice are modified to protect the privacy of the client.

[21]  Louis Ginzberg. *The Legends of the Jews, Vol. II* (Philadelphia: Jewish Publication Society, 1969), 4. My list summarizes a long list in this book, some items of which have little apparent connection with the text of Genesis.

[22]  NJPS TANAKH translates the second *bigdo* in 39:12 as "it." I replaced that with *his garment* in the citation above.

[23]  Sacks, *Not in God's Name*, 116-117.

## Chapter Two

[1]  Wenham. *Genesis 1–15*, 84.

[2]  Ramban. *Commentary on the Torah: Genesis* (New York: Shilo Publishing House, 1971) 169, citing Tanchuma *Lech Lecha*, 9, on Genesis 12:6.

[3]  The Jewish Encyclopedia notes there are three references to Messiah ben Joseph in Sukkah 52, "for the first of which R. Dosa (c. 250) is given as authority. In the last of these statements only his [Messiah ben Joseph's] name is mentioned, but the first two speak of the fate which he is to meet, namely, to fall in battle (as if alluding to a well-known tradition)." http://www.jewishencyclopedia.com/articles/10729-messiah#anchor16, accessed December 5, 2015.

4   See for example Genesis Rabbah, Vol II, on Genesis 32:6, also footnote
    on p. 698.
5   Matt 27:65-66; John 19:7.
6   Luke 23:2-3; John 19:12-16.
7   Craig S. Keener. *The Gospel of Matthew: A Socio-Rhetorical
    Commentary* (Grand Rapids: Eerdmans, 2009), 675.
8   Keener, 679.
9   Although the subject of some dispute among interpreters, Psalm 22,
    especially verses 15-19 [14-18 in Christian Bibles] clearly pictures a
    torturous death, with several details specifying crucifixion.
10  David Kinnaman, *unChristian: What a New Generation Really Thinks
    About Christianity... and Why It Matters* (Grand Rapids: Baker Books,
    2007), cited in http://www.goodreads.com/work/quotes/1041281-
    unchristian-what-a-new-generation-really-thinks-about-christianity-and,
    accessed 12/12/15.
11  http://www.tabletmag.com/jewish-life-and-religion/181524/why-i-left-
    my-synagogue, August 19, 2014, accessed 12/12/15.
12  http://jewishatheist.tumblr.com/post/59327799935/why-im-not-going-to-
    synagogue-this-year, dated August 25, 2013, accessed 12/12/15.
13  NT Wright, *What Saint Paul Really Said* (Grand Rapids: Eerdmans,
    1997), 83-84, cited in Douglas Harink, *Paul Among the Postliberals*
    (Grand Rapids: Brazos Press, 2003) 156.
14  CH Spurgeon, *The Treasury of David, Vol. 2, Part 1* (McLean, VA:
    MacDonald Publishing Co., n.d.), 481.
15  Sacks. *Not in God's Name*, 3, 9.
16  Minuchin, 47.
17  *JPS Torah Commentary*, ad loc., 306.

**Chapter Three**

1   Alan M. Dershowitz, *The Genesis of Justice: Ten Stories of Biblical
    Injustice That Led to the Ten Commandments and Modern Law* (New
    York: Warner Books, 2000), 187-188, 192.
2   Dershowitz (192-193) cites a midrash that explores the same idea. Joseph
    reveals himself to Benjamin in advance and tells him that if his brothers
    risk their lives to fight for him, "then shall I know that they have
    repented. . . . But if they forsake thee, I will keep thee, that thou shouldst
    remain with me."
3   *Hilchot Teshuvah* 2:1.
    http://www.torahlab.org/download/rambam_sourcesheet.pdf, accessed
    9/8/15.
4   Kass, 591.
5   Ibid., 602.

6   Friedman, 228–230.
7   Steinke, 78.
8   *JPS Torah Commentary*, 310.
9   *Kol HaTor* 2:39, R. Hillel Shaklover, trans. Rav Yechiel Bar-Lev. *The Voice of the Turtledove* (self-published, lulu.com). The book is ascribed to a direct disciple of the 18th-century Gaon of Vilna, but its authenticity is disputed. See https://en.wikipedia.org/wiki/Kol_HaTor. Even if it's a more recent work, however, it reflects much older portrayals of Messiah ben Joseph.
10  R. Nosson Scherman and R. Meir Zlotowitz, general eds., *Chumash: The Stone Edition* (Brooklyn: Artscroll, 1994), on Genesis 45:3, 253.
11  Feinberg, 160.
12  Ibid.
13  Friedman, *Generation*, 27, 208-210.
14  See 50:15-21.
15  JPS Torah commentary, 312.
16  Ibid., 313.
17  Wenham, *Genesis 16–50*, 449.

**Chapter Four**

1   Ron Chernow, *Washington: A Life* (New York: The Penguin Press, 2010), 802.
2   Ibid., 807–808.
3   Ibid., 131.
4   *JPS Torah commentary*, 323.
5   David Wein, "Jacob's Blessing." http://www.umjc.org/jacobs-blessing/, accessed 1/15/17.
6   I'm referencing the same Hebrew word, based on the root *SHACHAH*, in each of the appearances listed in this paragraph.
7   Kass, 648.
8   Russell Resnik, *Gateways to Torah: Joining the Ancient Conversation on the Weekly Portion* (Clarksville, MD: Lederer Books, 2000), 56. Rashi is a great Medieval Jewish commentator.
9   Michael Wyschogrod, "Israel, the Church, and Election" in *Abraham's Promise: Judaism and Jewish-Christian Relations* (Grand Rapids, MI: Eerdmans, 2004), pp. 186-187.
10  Kaminsky, 109.
11  Ibid., 25.
12  Sacks, *Not in God's Name*, 157.
13  *JPS Torah Commentary*, 246.
14  Ibid., 349.

[15]   http://www.rabbisacks.org/birth-forgiveness-vayigash-5775/#_ftnref1.
       Accessed 10/17/16. Emphasis in the original.

[16]   Sacks, *Not in God's Name*, 156.

[17]   *JPS Torah Commentary* 349.

[18]   Wenham, *Genesis 16–50*, 489.

[19]   J.R.R. Tolkien. *The Return of the King*, 331.

[20]   Ibid, 166.

[21]   Sacks, *Not in God's Name*, 157, emphasis added.

[22]   Dr. Fred Luskin, *Forgive for Good: A PROVEN Prescription for Health
       and Happiness* (New York: HarperOne, 2003), 110. Emphasis added.

[23]   I develop this idea in my book by the same title—*Divine Reversal: The
       Transforming Ethics of Jesus* (Clarksville, MD: Lederer Books, 2010)—
       the idea that the standards and values of the kingdom of God reverse the
       values of the dominant culture around us. The book develops this as is the
       theme of Yeshua's ethical teaching, which in turn is based on the ethical
       teaching of the Torah, as exemplified in the stories of Abraham and his
       descendants.

[24]   Rashi on Gen. 47:29, citing *Genesis Rabbah* 96:5.

[25]   *JPS Torah Commentary*, 351.

[26]   I owe this insight to my friend Catherine Fuerst, who helpfully read an early
       version of the manuscript.

## Conclusion

[1]   *Theological Wordbook*, comment on *bachar* (Bet Het Resh).

[2]   Wyschogrod, *Body of Faith*, 65.

[3]   Melkite Greek Archbishop Cyril Salim Bustros, cited by David P.
      Goldman, "Disappearing Middle Eastern Christians, Disappointing
      Bishops," 10/25/10.
      http://www.firstthings.com/onthesquare/2010/10/disappearing-middle-
      eastern-christians-disappointing-bishops, accessed 1/29/11.

[4]   In biblical usage, "Israel" normally refers to a people, the descendants of
      Abraham, Isaac and Jacob, not to a land or a state. I follow this usage in
      this book, and will generally say "land of Israel," or "state of Israel,"
      when I'm not speaking of Israel as a people.

[5]   Wyschogrod, *Abraham's Promise*, 184–185.

[6]   Ibid.

[7]   Here's how Jewish tradition enumerates 13 attributes within this passage:
      *Adonai* (1), *Adonai* (2) is God (3), merciful (4) and compassionate (5),
      slow to anger (6), rich in grace (7) and truth (8); showing grace to the
      thousandth generation (9), forgiving offenses (10), crimes (11) and sins
      (12); yet not exonerating the guilty (13). This last phrase is interpreted as
      "and who cleanses." God doesn't exonerate the guilty, but cleanses them

of their guilt when they repent, so this phrase is taken as a reference to his ultimate mercy. (*Chumash, The Stone Edition*, 509.)

[8] https://nimh.nih.gov/health/statistics/prevalence/major-depression-among-adults.shtml, accessed 10/24/16.

[9] https://www.nimh.nih.gov/health/statistics/prevalence/major-depression-among-adolescents.shtml, accessed 10/24/16.

[10] https://www.nimh.nih.gov/health/statistics/prevalence/any-anxiety-disorder-among-adults.shtml, https://www.nimh.nih.gov/health/statistics/prevalence/any-anxiety-disorder-among-children.shtml, accessed 1/22/17.

[11] https://www.barna.com/research/barna-trends-whats-new-whats-next/. Accessed 12/30/2016.

[12] Amy-Jill Levine, *Short Stories by Jesus* (New York: HarperOne, 2014), 184.

[13] Ibid., 208.

[14] Rabbi Israel Salanter, 1809-1883. See Morinis, Alan. *Everyday Holiness: The Jewish Spiritual Path of Mussar* (Boston: Trumpeter, 2008).

[15] The complete *Shema* includes this paragraph and two others, Deut. 11:13–21, and Num. 15:37–41.

*First Time in History!*

General Editor: Rabbi Barry Rubin
Theological Editor: Dr. John Fischer

## The Complete Jewish Study Bible

*Insights for Jews and Christians*

—Dr. David H. Stern

A One-of-a-Kind Study Bible that illuminates the Jewish background and context of God's word so it is more fully understandable. Uses the updated *Complete Jewish Bible* text by David H. Stern, including notes from the *Jewish New Testament Commentary* and contributions from Scholars listed below. 1990 pages.

< Hardcover Edition

| | | |
|---|---|---|
| Hardback | 978-1619708679 | $49.95 |
| Flexisoft | 978-1619708693 | $79.95 |
| Leather | 978-1619708709 | $139.95 |

Leather Edition w/color gift box   Flexisoft Edition w/color sleeve

### CONTRIBUTORS & SCHOLARS

| | | | |
|---|---|---|---|
| Rabbi Dr. Glenn Blank | Forbes | Rabbi Barney Kasdan | Rosenberg |
| Dr. Michael Brown | Rabbi Dr. David | Dr. Craig S. Keener | Rabbi Isaac Roussel |
| Rabbi Steven Bernstein | Friedman | Rabbi Elliot Klayman | Dr. Michael Rydelnik |
| Rabbi Joshua | Dr. Arnold | Jordan Gayle Levy | Dr. Jeffrey Seif |
| Brumbach | Fruchtenbaum | Dr. Ronald Moseley | Rabbi Tzahi Shapira |
| Rabbi Ron Corbett | Dr. John Garr | Rabbi Dr. Rich Nichol | Dr. David H. Stern |
| Pastor Ralph Finley | Pastor David Harris | Rabbi Mark J. Rantz | Dr. Bruce Stokes |
| Rabbi Dr. John Fischer | Benjamin Juster | Rabbi Russ Resnik | Dr. Tom Tribelhorn |
| Dr. Patrice Fischer | Rabbi Dr. Daniel Juster | Dr. Richard Robinson | Dr. Forrest Weiland |
| Rebbitzen Malkah | Dr. Walter C. Kaiser | Rabbi Dr. Jacob | Dr. Marvin Wilson |

### QUOTES BY JEWISH SCHOLARS & SAGES

Dr. Daniel Boyarin
Dr. Amy-Jill Levine
Rabbi Jonathan Sacks
Rabbi Gamaliel
Rabbi Hillel
Rabbi Shammai
Rabbi Akiva
Maimonides
and many more

## Complete Jewish Bible: *An English Version*

—Dr. David H. Stern (Available March 2017)

Now, the most widely used Messianic Jewish Bible around the world, has updated text with introductions added to each book, written from a biblically Jewish perspective. The CJB is a unified Jewish book, a version for Jews and non-Jews alike; to connect Jews with the Jewishness of the Messiah, and non-Jews with their Jewish roots. Names and terms are returned to their original Hebrew and presented in easy-to-understand transliterations, enabling the reader to say them the way *Yeshua* (Jesus) did! 1728 pages.

| | | |
|---|---|---|
| Paperback | 978-1936716845 | $29.95 |
| Hardcover | 978-1936716852 | $34.95 |
| Flexisoft Cover | 978-1936716869 | $49.95 |

## Jewish New Testament
### —Dr. David H. Stern

*The New Testament* is a Jewish book, written by Jews, initially for Jews. Its central figure was a Jew. His followers were all Jews; yet no other version really communicates its original, essential Jewishness. Uses neutral terms and Hebrew names. Highlights Jewish references and corrects mistranslations. Freshly translated into English from Greek, this is a must read to learn about first-century faith. 436 pages

| | | | |
|---|---|---|---|
| Hardback | 978-9653590069 | **JB02** | $19.99 |
| Paperback | 978-9653590038 | **JB01** | $14.99 |
| Spanish | 978-1936716272 | **JB17** | $24.99 |

Also available in French, German, Polish, Portuguese and Russian.

## Jewish New Testament Commentary
### —Dr. David H. Stern

This companion to the *Jewish New Testament* enhances Bible study. Passages and expressions are explained in their original cultural context. 15 years of research. 960 pages.

| | | | |
|---|---|---|---|
| Hardback | 978-9653590083 | **JB06** | $34.99 |
| Paperback | 978-9653590113 | **JB10** | $29.99 |

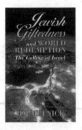

## Will the Nazi Eagle Rise Again?
*What the Church Needs to Know about BDS and Other Forces of Anti-Semitism*
### –David Friedman, Ph.D.

This is the right book at the right time. exposing the roots of Anti-Semitism being resurrected in our days, especially in our Christian Church.
—Dr. Hans-Jörg Kagi, Teacher, Theologian, Basle, Switzerland
Timely and important response to the dangerous hatred of the State of Israel that is growing in society and in the Church.
—Michael Rydelnik, Prof. of Jewish Studies, Moody Bible Inst., Chicago, Ill.
Israel is not an apartheid state and bears absolutely no resemblance to the institutionalized racial oppression that I lived under in South Africa. I am deeply offended by this comparison.
—Luba Mayekiso, Africa for Israel Christian Coalition, Republic of South Africa
Paperback (278 Pages)    978-1936716876    $19.99

## Jewish Giftedness & World Redemption
### *The Calling of Israel*
### –Jim Melnick

*All things are mortal but the Jew; all other forces pass, but he remains. What is the secret of his immortality?*
—Mark Twain, Concerning the Jews, *Harper's Magazine*, September, 1899.

*The most comprehensive research of the unique achievements of the Jewish people. The author comes up with the only reason that makes sense of this mystery.*
—Daniel C. Juster, Th.D., Restoration from Zion of Tikkun International
Paperback (280 Pages)    978-1-936716-88-3    $24.99

## Messianic Judaism *A Modern Movement With an Ancient Past*
—David H. Stern

An updated discussion of the history, ideology, theology and program for Messianic Judaism. A challenge to both Jews and non-Jews who honor Yeshua to catch the vision of Messianic Judaism. 312 pages

|  | 978-1880226339 | **LB62** | $17.99 |

## Restoring the Jewishness of the Gospel
*A Message for Christians*
—David H. Stern

Introduces Christians to the Jewish roots of their faith, challenges some conventional ideas, and raises some neglected questions: How are both the Jews and "the Church" God's people? Is the Law of Moses in force today? Filled with insight! Endorsed by Dr. Darrell L. Bock. 110 pages

| English | 978-1880226667 | **LB70** | $9.99 |
| Spanish | 978-9653590175 | **JB14** | $9.99 |

## Come and Worship *Ways to Worship from the Hebrew Scriptures*
—Compiled by Barbara D. Malda

We were created to worship. God has graciously given us many ways to express our praise to him. Each way fits a different situation or moment in life, yet all are intended to bring honor and glory to him. When we believe that he is who he says he is [see *His Names are Wonderful!*] and that his Word is true, worship flows naturally from our hearts to his. Softcover, 128 pages.

|  | 978-1936716678 | **LB88** | $9.99 |

## His Names Are Wonderful
*Getting to Know God Through His Hebrew Names*
—Elizabeth L. Vander Meulen and Barbara D. Malda

In Hebrew thought, names did more than identify people; they revealed their nature. God's identity is expressed not in one name, but in many. This book will help readers know God better as they uncover the truths in his Hebrew names. 160 pages.

|  | 978-1880226308 | **LB58** | $9.99 |

## The Return of the Kosher Pig *The Divine Messiah in Jewish Thought*
—Rabbi Tzahi Shapira

The subject of Messiah fills many pages of rabbinic writings. Hidden in those pages is a little known concept that the Messiah has the same authority given to God. Based on the Scriptures and traditional rabbinic writings, this book shows the deity of Yeshua from a new perspective. You will see that the rabbis of old expected the Messiah to be divine. Softcover, 352 pages.

*"One of the most interesting and learned tomes I have ever read. Contained within its pages is much with which I agree, some with which I disagree, and much about which I never thought. Rabbi Shapria's remarkable book cannot be ignored."*

—Dr. Paige Patterson, President, Southwest Baptist Theological Seminary

|  | 978-1936716456 | **LB81** | $ 39.99 |

## Proverbial Wisdom & Common Sense

*A Messianic Commentary*

—Derek Leman

A Messianic Jewish Approach to Today's Issues from the Proverbs
A devotional style commentary, divided into chapters suitable for daily
reading. An encyclopedia of practical advice on topics relevant to everyone.
248 pages

Paperback 978-1880226780 **LB98** $19.99

## Matthew Presents Yeshua, King Messiah *A Messianic Commentary*

—Rabbi Barney Kasdan

Few commentators are able to truly present Yeshua in his Jewish context.
Most don't understand his background, his family, even his religion, and
consequently really don't understand who he truly is. This commentator is
well versed with first-century Jewish practices and thought, as well as the
historical and cultural setting of the day, and the 'traditions of the Elders'
that Yeshua so often spoke about. Get to know Yeshua, the King, through
the writing of another rabbi, Barney Kasdan. 448 pages

978-1936716265 **LB76** $29.99

## Rabbi Paul Enlightens the Ephesians on Walking with Messiah Yeshua

*A Messianic Commentary*

—Rabbi Barney Kasdan

The Ephesian were a diverse group of Jews and Gentiles, united together in
Messiah. They definitely had an impact on the first century world in which
they lived. But the Rabbi was not just writing to that local group. What is
Paul saying to us? 160 pages.

Paperback 978-11936716821 **LB99** $17.99

## James the Just Presents Application of Torah

*A Messianic Commentary*

—Dr. David Friedman

James (Jacob) one of the Epistles written to first century Jewish followers of
Yeshua. Dr. David Friedman, a former Professor of the Israel Bible Institute
has shed new light for Christians from this very important letter.

978-1936716449 **LB82** $14.99

## Jude On Faith and the Destructive Influence of Heresy

*A Messianic Commentary*

—Rabbi Joshua Brumbach

Almost no other canonical book has been as neglected and overlooked as
the Epistle of Jude. This little book may be small, but it has a big message
that is even more relevant today as when it was originally written.

978-1-936716-78-4 **LB97** $14.99

## Psalms & Proverbs *Tehillim* תְּהִלִּים-*Mishlei* מִשְׁלֵי
—Translated by Dr. David Stern

Contemplate the power in these words anytime, anywhere: Psalms-*Tehillim* offers uplifting words of praise and gratitude, keeping us focused with the right attitude; Proverbs-*Mishlei* gives us the wisdom for daily living, renewing our minds by leading us to examine our actions, to discern good from evil, and to decide freely to do the good. Makes a wonderful and meaningful gift. Softcover, 224 pages.

978-1936716692    LB90    $9.99

## At the Feet of Rabbi Gamaliel
*Rabbinic Influence in Paul's Teachings*
—David Friedman, Ph.D.

Paul (Shaul) was on the "fast track" to becoming a sage and Sanhedrin judge, describing himself as passionate for the Torah and the traditions of the fathers, typical for an aspiring Pharisee: "...trained at the feet of Gamaliel in every detail of the Torah of our forefathers. I was a zealot for God, as all of you are today" (Acts 22.3, CJB). Did Shaul's teachings reflect Rabbi Gamaliel's instructions? Did Paul continue to value the Torah and Pharisaic tradition? Did Paul create a 'New' Theology? The results of the research within these pages and its conclusion may surprise you. Softcover, 100 pages.

978-1936716753    **LB95**    $8.99

## Debranding God *Revealing His True Essence*
—Eduardo Stein

The process of 'debranding' God is to remove all the labels and fads that prompt us to understand him as a supplier and ourselves as the most demanding of customers. Changing our perception of God also changes our perception of ourselves. In knowing who we are in relationship to God, we discover his, and our, true essence. Softcover, 252 pages.

978-1936716708    **LB91**    $16.99

## Under the Fig Tree *Messianic Thought Through the Hebrew Calendar*
—Patrick Gabriel Lumbroso

Take a daily devotional journey into the Word of God through the Hebrew Calendar and the Biblical Feasts. Learn deeper meaning of the Scriptures through Hebraic thought. Beautifully written and a source for inspiration to draw closer to Adonai every day. Softcover, 407 pages.

978-1936716760    **LB96**    $25.99

## Under the Vine *Messianic Thought Through the Hebrew Calendar*
—Patrick Gabriel Lumbroso

Journey daily through the Hebrew Calendar and Biblical Feasts into the B'rit Hadashah (New Testament) Scriptures as they are put in their rightful context, bringing Judaism alive in it's full beauty. Messianic faith was the motor and what gave substance to Abraham's new beliefs, hope to Job, trust to Isaac, vision to Jacob, resilience to Joseph, courage to David, wisdom to Solomon, knowledge to Daniel, and divine Messianic authority to Yeshua. Softcover, 412 pages.

978-1936716654    **LB87**    $25.99

## The Revolt of Rabbi Morris Cohen
*Exploring the Passion & Piety of a Modern-day Pharisee*
—Anthony Cardinale

A brilliant school psychologist, Rabbi Morris Cohen went on a one-man strike to protest the systematic mislabeling of slow learning pupils as "Learning Disabled" (to extract special education money from the state). His disciplinary hearing, based on the transcript, is a hilarious read! This effusive, garrulous man with an irresistible sense of humor lost his job, but achieved a major historic victory causing the reform of the billion-dollar special education program. Enter into the mind of an eighth-generation Orthodox rabbi to see how he deals spiritually with the loss of everything, even the love of his children. This modern-day Pharisee discovered a trusted friend in the author (a born again believer in Jesus) with whom he could openly struggle over Rabbinic Judaism as well as the concept of Jesus (Yeshua) as Messiah. Softcover, 320 pages.

978-1936716722    **LB92**    $19.99

---

## Stories of Yeshua
—Jim Reimann, Illustrator Julia Filipone-Erez

Children's Bible Storybook with four stories about Yeshua (Jesus).
*Yeshua is Born: The Bethlehem Story* based on Lk 1:26-35 & 2:1-20; *Yeshua and Nicodemus in Jerusalem* based on Jn 3:1-16; *Yeshua Loves the Little Children of the World* based on Matthew 18:1–6 & 19:13–15; *Yeshua is Alive-The Empty Tomb in Jerusalem* based on Matthew 26:17-56, Jn 19:16-20:18, Lk 24:50-53. Ages 3-7, Softcover, 48 pages.

978-1936716685    **LB89**    $14.99

---

## To the Ends of the Earth – How the First Jewish Followers of Yeshua Transformed the Ancient World
— Dr. Jeffrey Seif

Everyone knows that the first followers of Yeshua were Jews, and that Christianity was very Jewish for the first 50 to 100 years. It's a known fact that there were many congregations made up mostly of Jews, although the false perception today is, that in the second century they disappeared. Dr. Seif reveals the truth of what happened to them and how these early Messianic Jews influenced and transformed the behavior of the known world at that time.

978-1936716463    **LB83**    $17.99

---

## Passion for Israel: *A Short History of the Evangelical Church's Support of Israel and the Jewish People*
—Dan Juster

History reveals a special commitment of Christians to the Jews as God's still elect people, but the terrible atrocities committed against the Jews by so-called Christians have overshadowed the many good deeds that have been performed. This important history needs to be told to help heal the wounds and to inspire more Christians to stand together in support of Israel.

978-1936716401    **LB78**    $9.99

## Jewish Roots and Foundations of the Scriptures I & II
—John Fischer, Th.D, Ph.D.

An outstanding evangelical leader once said: "There is something shallow about a Christianity that has lost its Jewish roots." A beautiful painting is a careful interweaving of a number of elements. Among other things, there are the background, the foreground and the subject. Discovering the roots of your faith is a little like appreciating the various parts of a painting. In the background is the panorama of preparation and pictures found in the Old Testament. In the foreground is the landscape and light of the first century Jewish setting. All of this is intricately connected with and highlights the subject—which becomes the flowering of all these aspects—the coming of God to earth and what that means for us. Discovering and appreciating your roots in this way broadens, deepens and enriches your faith and your understanding of Scripture. This audio is 32 hours of live class instruction - audio is clear and easy to understand.

9781936716623   **LCD03 / LCD04**   $49.99 each

## The Gospels in their Jewish Context
—John Fischer, Th.D, Ph.D.

An examination of the Jewish background and nature of the Gospels in their contemporary political, cultural and historical settings, emphasizing each gospel's special literary presentation of Yeshua, and highlighting the cultural and religious contexts necessary for understanding each of the gospels. 32 hours of audio/video instruction on MP3-DVD and pdf of syllabus.

978-1936716241   **LCD01**   $49.99

## The Epistles from a Jewish Perspective
—John Fischer, Th.D, Ph.D.

An examination of the relationship of Rabbi Shaul (the Apostle Paul) and the Apostles to their Jewish contemporaries and environment; surveys their Jewish practices, teaching, controversy with the religious leaders, and many critical passages, with emphasis on the Jewish nature, content, and background of these letters. 32 hours of audio/video instruction on MP3-DVD and pdf of syllabus.

978-1936716258   **LCD02**   $49.99

## The Red Heifer *A Jewish Cry for Messiah*
—Anthony Cardinale

Award-winning journalist and playwright Anthony Cardinale has traveled extensively in Israel, and recounts here his interviews with Orthodox rabbis, secular Israelis, and Palestinian Arabs about the current search for a red heifer by Jewish radicals wishing to rebuild the Temple and bring the Messiah. These real-life interviews are interwoven within an engaging and dramatic fictional portrayal of the diverse people of Israel and how they would react should that red heifer be found. Readers will find themselves in the Land, where they can hear learned rabbis and ordinary Israelis talking about the red heifer and dealing with all the related issues and the imminent coming and identity of Messiah.

978-1936716470   LB79   $19.99

## The Borough Park Papers
—Multiple Authors

As you read the New Testament, you "overhear" debates first-century Messianic Jews had about critical issues, e.g. Gentiles being "allowed" into the Messianic kingdom (Acts 15). Similarly, you're now invited to "listen in" as leading twenty-first century Messianic Jewish theologians discuss critical issues facing us today. Some ideas may not fit into your previously held pre-suppositions or pre-conceptions. Indeed, you may find some paradigm shifting in your thinking. We want to share the thoughts of these thinkers with you, our family in the Messiah.

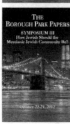

### Symposium I:
*The Gospel and the Jewish People*
248 pages

|  |  |  |
|---|---|---|
| 978-1936716593 | LB84 | $39.95 |

### Symposium II:
*The Deity of Messiah and the Mystery of God*
211 pages

|  |  |  |
|---|---|---|
| 978-1936716609 | LB85 | $39.95 |

### Symposium III:
*How Jewish Should the Messianic Community Be?*

|  |  |  |
|---|---|---|
| 978-1936716616 | LB86 | $39.95 |

---

## On The Way to Emmaus: *Searching the Messianic Prophecies*
—Dr. Jacques Doukhan

An outstanding compilation of the most critical Messianic prophecies by a renowned conservative Christian Scholar, drawing on material from the Bible, Rabbinic sources, Dead Sea Scrolls, and more.

|  |  |  |
|---|---|---|
| 978-1936716432 | LB80 | $14.99 |

---

## Yeshua *A Guide to the Real Jesus and the Original Church*
—Dr. Ron Moseley

Opens up the history of the Jewish roots of the Christian faith. Illuminates the Jewish background of Yeshua and the Church and never flinches from showing "Jesus was a Jew, who was born, lived, and died, within first century Judaism." Explains idioms in the New Testament. Endorsed by Dr. Brad Young and Dr. Marvin Wilson. 213 pages.

|  |  |  |
|---|---|---|
| 978-1880226681 | **LB29** | $12.99 |

## Gateways to Torah *Joining the Ancient Conversation on the Weekly Portion*
—Rabbi Russell Resnik

From before the days of Messiah until today, Jewish people have read from and discussed a prescribed portion of the Pentateuch each week. Now, a Messianic Jewish Rabbi, Russell Resnik, brings another perspective on the Torah, that of a Messianic Jew. 246 pages.

978-1880226889    **LB42**    $15.99

## Creation to Completion *A Guide to Life's Journey from the Five Books of Moses*
—Rabbi Russell Resnik

Endorsed by Coach Bill McCartney, Founder of Promise Keepers & Road to Jerusalem: "Paul urged Timothy to study the Scriptures (2 Tim. 3:16), advising him to apply its teachings to all aspects of his life. Since there was no New Testament then, this rabbi/apostle was convinced that his disciple would profit from studying the Torah, the Five Books of Moses, and the Old Testament. Now, Rabbi Resnik has written a warm devotional commentary that will help you understand and apply the Law of Moses to your life in a practical way." 256 pages

978-1880226322    **LB61**    $14.99

## Walk Genesis!   Walk Exodus!   Walk Leviticus!   Walk Numbers! Walk Deuteronomy!
*Messianic Jewish Devotional Commentaries*
—Jeffrey Enoch Feinberg, Ph.D.

Using the weekly synagogue readings, Dr. Jeffrey Feinberg has put together some very valuable material in his "Walk" series. Each section includes a short Hebrew lesson (for the non-Hebrew speaker), key concepts, an excellent overview of the portion, and some practical applications. Can be used as a daily devotional as well as a Bible study tool.

| | | | | |
|---|---|---|---|---|
| *Walk Genesis!* | 238 pages | 978-1880226759 | **LB34** | $12.99 |
| *Walk Exodus!* | 224 pages | 978-1880226872 | **LB40** | $12.99 |
| *Walk Leviticus!* | 208 pages | 978-1880226926 | **LB45** | $12.99 |
| *Walk Numbers!* | 211 pages | 978-1880226995 | **LB48** | $12.99 |
| *Walk Deuteronomy!* | 231 pages | 978-1880226186 | **LB51** | $12.99 |
| *SPECIAL! Five-book Walk!* | | 5 Book Set **Save $10** | **LK28** | $54.99 |

## Good News According To Matthew
—Dr. Henry Einspruch

English translation with quotations from the Tanakh (Old Testament) capitalized and printed in Hebrew. Helpful notations are included. Lovely black and white illustrations throughout the book. 86 pages.

|  | 978-1880226025 | **LB03** | $4.99 |
| Also available in Yiddish. | | **LB02** | $4.99 |

## They Loved the Torah *What Yeshua's First Followers Really Thought About the Law*
—Dr. David Friedman

Although many Jews believe that Paul taught against the Law, this book disproves that notion. An excellent case for his premise that all the first followers of the Messiah were not only Torah-observant, but also desired to spread their love for God's entire Word to the gentiles to whom they preached. 144 pages. Endorsed by Dr. David Stern, Ariel Berkowitz, Rabbi Dr. Stuart Dauermann & Dr. John Fischer.

978-1880226940 **LB47** $9.99

## The Distortion *2000 Years of Misrepresenting the Relationship Between Jesus the Messiah and the Jewish People*
—Dr. John Fischer & Dr. Patrice Fischer

Did the Jews kill Jesus? Did they really reject him? With the rise of global anti–Semitism, it is important to understand what the Gospels teach about the relationship between Jewish people and their Messiah. 2000 years of distortion have made this difficult. Learn how the distortion began and continues to this day and what you can do to change it. 126 pages. Endorsed by Dr. Ruth Fleischer, Rabbi Russell Resnik, Dr. Daniel C. Juster, Dr. Michael Rydelnik.

978-1880226254 **LB54** $11.99

---

# eBooks Now Available!
*All books are available as ebooks
for your favorite reader*

Visit www.messianicjewish.net for direct links to these readers
for each available eBook.

## God's Appointed Times *A Practical Guide to Understanding and Celebrating the Biblical Holidays* – **New Edition.**

—Rabbi Barney Kasdan

The Biblical Holy Days teach us about the nature of God and his plan for mankind, and can be a source of God's blessing for all believers–Jews and Gentiles–today. Includes historical background, traditional Jewish observance, New Testament relevance, and prophetic significance, plus music, crafts and holiday recipes. 145 pages.

| | | | |
|---|---|---|---|
| English | 978-1880226353 | **LB63** | $12.99 |
| Spanish | 978-1880226391 | **LB59** | $12.99 |

## God's Appointed Customs *A Messianic Jewish Guide to the Biblical Lifecycle and Lifestyle*

— Rabbi Barney Kasdan

Explains how biblical customs are often the missing key to unlocking the depths of Scripture. Discusses circumcision, the Jewish wedding, and many more customs mentioned in the New Testament. Companion to *God's Appointed Times*. 170 pages.

| | | | |
|---|---|---|---|
| English | 978-1880226636 | **LB26** | $12.99 |
| Spanish | 978-1880226551 | **LB60** | $12.99 |

## Celebrations of the Bible *A Messianic Children's Curriculum*

Did you know that each Old Testament feast or festival finds its fulfillment in the New? They enrich the lives of people who experience and enjoy them. Our popular curriculum for children is in a brand new, user-friendly format. The lay-flat at binding allows you to easily reproduce handouts and worksheets. Celebrations of the Bible has been used by congregations, Sunday schools, ministries, homeschoolers, and individuals to teach children about the biblical festivals. Each of these holidays are presented for Preschool (2-K), Primary (Grades 1-3), Junior (Grades 4-6), and Children's Worship/Special Services. 208 pages.

| | | |
|---|---|---|
| 978-1880226261 | **LB55** | $24.99 |

## Passover: *The Key That Unlocks the Book of Revelation*

—Daniel C. Juster, Th.D.

Is there any more enigmatic book of the Bible than Revelation? Controversy concerning its meaning has surrounded it back to the first century. Today, the arguments continue. Yet, Dan Juster has given us the key that unlocks the entire book—the events and circumstances of the Passover/Exodus. By interpreting Revelation through the lens of Exodus, Dan Juster provides a unified overview that helps us read Revelation as it was always meant to be read, as a drama of spiritual conflict, deliverance, and above all, worship. He also shows how this final drama, fulfilled in Messiah, resonates with the Torah and all of God's Word. — Russ Resnik, Executive Director, Union of Messianic Jewish Congregations.

| | | |
|---|---|---|
| 978-1936716210 | **LB74** | $10.99 |

## The Messianic Passover Haggadah
*Revised and Updated*
—Rabbi Barry Rubin and Steffi Rubin.

Guides you through the traditional Passover seder dinner, step-by-step. Not only does this observance remind us of our rescue from Egyptian bondage, but, we remember Messiah's last supper, a Passover seder. The theme of redemption is seen throughout the evening. What's so unique about our Haggadah is the focus on Yeshua (Jesus) the Messiah and his teaching, especially on his last night in the upper room. 36 pages.

| | | | |
|---|---|---|---|
| English | 978-1880226292 | **LB57** | $4.99 |
| Spanish | 978-1880226599 | **LBSP01** | $4.99 |

## The Messianic Passover Seder Preparation Guide
Includes recipes, blessings and songs. 19 pages.

| | | | |
|---|---|---|---|
| English | 978-1880226247 | **LB10** | $2.99 |
| Spanish | 978-1880226728 | **LBSP02** | $2.99 |

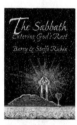

## The Sabbath *Entering God's Rest*
—Barry Rubin & Steffi Rubin

Even if you've never celebrated Shabbat before, this book will guide you into the rest God has for all who would enter in—Jews and non-Jews. Contains prayers, music, recipes; in short, everything you need to enjoy the Sabbath, even how to observe havdalah, the closing ceremony of the Sabbath. Also discusses the Saturday or Sunday controversy. 48 pages.

978-1880226742    **LB32**    $6.99

## Havdalah *The Ceremony that Completes the Sabbath*
—Dr. Neal & Jamie Lash

The Sabbath ends with this short, yet equally sweet ceremony called havdalah (separation). This ceremony reminds us to be a light and a sweet fragrance in this world of darkness as we carry the peace, rest, joy and love of the Sabbath into the work week. 28 pages.

978-1880226605    **LB69**    $4.99

## Dedicate and Celebrate!
*A Messianic Jewish Guide to Hanukkah*
—Barry Rubin & Family

Hanukkah means "dedication" — a theme of significance for Jews and Christians. Discussing its historical background, its modern-day customs, deep meaning for all of God's people, this little book covers all the how-tos! Recipes, music, and prayers for lighting the menorah, all included! 32 pages.

978-1880226834    **LB36**    $4.99

## The Conversation
### *An Intimate Journal of the Emmaus Encounter*
—Judy Salisbury

*"Then beginning with Moses and with all the prophets, He explained to them the things concerning Himself in all the Scriptures."* Luke 24:27
If you've ever wondered what that conversation must have been like, this captivating book takes you there.

*"The Conversation brings to life that famous encounter between the two disciples and our Lord Jesus on the road to Emmaus. While it is based in part on an imaginative reconstruction, it is filled with the throbbing pulse of the excitement of the sensational impact that our Lord's resurrection should have on all of our lives."* ~ Dr. Walter Kaiser President Emeritus Gordon-Conwell Theological Seminary. Hardcover 120 pages.

| | | | |
|---|---|---|---|
| Hardcover | 978-1936716173 | **LB73** | $14.99 |
| Paperback | 978-1936716364 | **LB77** | $9.99 |

---

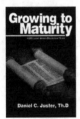

## Growing to Maturity
### *A Messianic Jewish Discipleship Guide*
—Daniel C. Juster, Th.D.

This discipleship series presents first steps of understanding and spiritual practice, tailored for the Jewish believer. It's purpose is to aid the believer in living according to Yeshua's will as a disciple, one who has learned the example of his teacher. The course is structured according to recent advances in individualized educational instruction. Discipleship is serious business and the material is geared for serious study and reflection. Each chapter is divided into short sections followed by study questions. 256 pages.

| | | |
|---|---|---|
| 978-1936716227 | **LB75** | $19.99 |

## Growing to Maturity Primer: *A Messianic Jewish Discipleship Workbook*
—Daniel C. Juster, Th.D.

A basic book of material in question and answer form. Usable by everyone. 60 pages.

| | | |
|---|---|---|
| 978-0961455507 | **TB16** | $7.99 |

---

## Conveying Our Heritage A Messianic Jewish Guide to Home Practice
—Daniel C. Juster, Th.D. Patricia A. Juster

Throughout history the heritage of faith has been conveyed within the family and the congregation. The first institution in the Bible is the family and only the family can raise children with an adequate appreciation of our faith and heritage. This guide exists to help families learn how to pass on the heritage of spiritual Messianic Jewish life. Softcover, 86 pages

| | | |
|---|---|---|
| 978-1936716739 | **LB93** | $8.99 |

---

## That They May Be One *A Brief Review of Church Restoration Movements and Their Connection to the Jewish People*
—Daniel Juster, Th.D

Something prophetic and momentous is happening. The Church is finally fully grasping its relationship to Israel and the Jewish people. Author describes the restoration movements in Church history and how they connected to Israel and the Jewish people. Each one contributed in some way—some more, some less—toward the ultimate unity between Jews and Gentiles. Predicted in the Old Testament and fulfilled in the New, Juster believes this plan of God finds its full expression in Messianic Judaism. He may be right. See what you think as you read *That They May Be One*. 100 pages.

978-1880226711    LB71    $9.99

---

## The Greatest Commandment
*How the Sh'ma Leads to More Love in Your Life*
—Irene Lipson

"What is the greatest commandment?" Yeshua was asked. His reply—"Hear, O Israel, the Lord our God, the Lord is one, and you are to love Adonai your God with all your heart, with all your soul, with all your understanding, and all your strength." A superb book explaining each word so the meaning can be fully grasped and lived. Endorsed by Elliot Klayman, Susan Perlman, & Robert Stearns. 175 pages.

978-1880226360    LB65    $12.99

---

## Blessing the King of the Universe
*Transforming Your Life Through the Practice of Biblical Praise*
—Irene Lipson

Insights into the ancient biblical practice of blessing God are offered clearly and practically. With examples from Scripture and Jewish tradition, this book teaches the biblical formula used by men and women of the Bible, including the Messiah; points to new ways and reasons to praise the Lord; and explains more about the Jewish roots of the faith. Endorsed by Rabbi Barney Kasdan, Dr. Mitch Glaser, & Rabbi Dr. Dan Cohn-Sherbok. 144 pages.

978-1880226797    LB53    $11.99

---

## You Bring the Bagels, I'll Bring the Gospel
*Sharing the Messiah with Your Jewish Neighbor*
*Revised Edition—Now with Study Questions*
—Rabbi Barry Rubin

This "how-to-witness-to-Jewish-people" book is an orderly presentation of everything you need to share the Messiah with a Jewish friend. Includes Messianic prophecies, Jewish objections to believing, sensitivities in your witness, words to avoid. A "must read" for all who care about the Jewish people. Good for individual or group study. Used in Bible schools. Endorsed by Harold A. Sevener, Dr. Walter C. Kaiser, Dr. Erwin J. Kolb and Dr. Arthur F. Glasser. 253 pages.

English                 978-1880226650 **LB13**    $12.99
Te Tengo Buenas Noticias   978-0829724103 **OBSP02** $14.99

---

## Making Eye Contact With God
### *A Weekly Devotional for Women*
—Terri Gillespie

What kind of eyes do you have? Are they downcast and sad? Are they full of God's joy and passion? See yourself through the eyes of God. Using real life anecdotes, combined with scripture, the author reveals God's heart for women everywhere, as she softly speaks of the ways in which women see God. Endorsed by prominent authors: Dr. Angela Hunt, Wanda Dyson and Kathryn Mackel. 247 pages, hardcover.

978-1880226513    **LB68**    $19.99

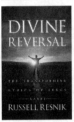

## Divine Reversal
### *The Transforming Ethics of Jesus*
—Rabbi Russell Resnik

In the Old Testament, God often reversed the plans of man. Yeshua's ethics continue this theme. Following his path transforms one's life from within, revealing the source of true happiness, forgiveness, reconciliation, fidelity and love. From the introduction, "As a Jewish teacher, Jesus doesn't separate matters of theology from practice. His teaching is consistently practical, ethical, and applicable to real life, even two thousand years after it was originally given." Endorsed by Jonathan Bernis, Dr. Daniel C. Juster, Dr. Jeffrey L. Seif, and Dr Darrell Bock. 206 pages

978-1880226803    **LB72**    $12.99

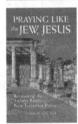

## Praying Like the Jew, Jesus
### *Recovering the Ancient Roots of New Testament Prayer*
—Dr. Timothy P. Jones

This eye-opening book reveals the Jewish background of many of Yeshua's prayers. Historical vignettes "transport" you to the times of Yeshua so you can grasp the full meaning of Messiah's prayers. Unique devotional thoughts and meditations, presented in down-to-earth language, provide inspiration for a more meaningful prayer life and help you draw closer to God. Endorsed by Mark Galli, James W. Goll, Rev. Robert Stearns, James F. Strange, and Dr. John Fischer. 144 pages.

978-1880226285    **LB56**    $9.99

## Growing Your Olive Tree Marriage *A Guide for Couples from Two Traditions*
—David J. Rudolph

One partner is Jewish; the other is Christian. Do they celebrate Hanukkah, Christmas or both? Do they worship in a church or a synagogue? How will the children be raised? This is the first book from a biblical perspective that addresses the concerns of intermarried couples, offering a godly solution. Includes highlights of interviews with intermarried couples. Endorsed by Walter C. Kaiser, Jr., Rabbi Dan Cohn-Sherbok, Jonathan Settel, Dr. Mitchell Glaser & Natalie Sirota. 224 pages.

978-1880226179    **LB50**    $12.99

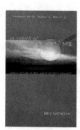

## In Search of the Silver Lining *Where is God in the Midst of Life's Storms?*
—Jerry Gramckow

When faced with suffering, what are your choices? Storms have always raged. And people have either perished in their wake or risen above the tempests, shaping history by their responses…new storms are on the horizon. How will we deal with them? How will we shape history or those who follow us? The answer lies in how we view God in the midst of the storms. Endorsed by Joseph C. Aldrich, Ray Beeson, Dr. Daniel Juster. 176 pages.

978-1880226865 **LB39** $10.99

## The Voice of the Lord *Messianic Jewish Daily Devotional*
—Edited by David J. Rudolph

Brings insight into the Jewish Scriptures—both Old and New Testaments. Twenty-two prominent Messianic contributors provide practical ways to apply biblical truth. Start your day with this unique resource. Explanatory notes. Perfect companion to the Complete Jewish Bible (see page 2). Endorsed by Edith Schaeffer, Dr. Arthur F. Glaser, Dr. Michael L. Brown, Mitch Glaser and Moishe Rosen. 416 pages.

9781880226704 **LB31** $19.99

## Kingdom Relationships *God's Laws for the Community of Faith*
—Dr. Ron Moseley

Dr. Ron Moseley's Yeshua: A Guide to the Real Jesus and the Original Church has taught thousands of people about the Jewishness of not only Yeshua, but of the first followers of the Messiah.

In this work, Moseley focuses on the teaching of Torah -- the Five Books of Moses -- tapping into truths that greatly help modern-day members of the community of faith. 64 pages.

978-1880226841 **LB37** $8.99

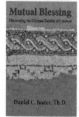

## Mutual Blessing *Discovering the Ultimate Destiny of Creation*
—Daniel C. Juster

To truly love as God loves is to see the wonder and richness of the distinct differences in all of creation and his natural order of interdependence. This is the way to mutual blessing and the discovery of the ultimate destiny of creation. Learn how to become enriched and blessed as you enrich and bless others and all that is around you! Softcover, 135 pages.

978-1936716746 **LB94** $9.99

## Train Up A Child *Successful Parenting For The Next Generation*
—Dr. Daniel L. Switzer

The author, former principal of Ets Chaiyim Messianic Jewish Day School, and father of four, combines solid biblical teaching with Jewish sources on child raising, focusing on the biblical holy days, giving fresh insight into fulfilling the role of parent. 188 pages. Endorsed by Dr. David J. Rudolph, Paul Lieberman, and Dr. David H. Stern.

978-1880226377 **LB64** $12.99

## Fire on the Mountain - *Past Renewals, Present Revivals and the Coming Return of Israel*
—Dr. Louis Goldberg

The term "revival" is often used to describe a person or congregation turning to God. Is this something that "just happens," or can it be brought about? Dr. Louis Goldberg, author and former professor of Hebrew and Jewish Studies at Moody Bible Institute, examines real revivals that took place in Bible times and applies them to today. 268 pages.

978-1880226858    **LB38**    $15.99

---

## Voices of Messianic Judaism *Confronting Critical Issues Facing a Maturing Movement*
—General Editor Rabbi Dan Cohn-Sherbok

Many of the best minds of the Messianic Jewish movement contributed their thoughts to this collection of 29 substantive articles. Challenging questions are debated: The involvement of Gentiles in Messianic Judaism? How should outreach be accomplished? Liturgy or not? Intermarriage? 256 pages.

978-1880226933    **LB46**    $15.99

---

## The Enduring Paradox *Exploratory Essays in Messianic Judaism*
—General Editor Dr. John Fischer

Yeshua and his Jewish followers began a new movement—Messianic Judaism—2,000 years ago. In the 20th century, it was reborn. Now, at the beginning of the 21st century, it is maturing. Twelve essays from top contributors to the theology of this vital movement of God, including: Dr. Walter C. Kaiser, Dr. David H. Stern, and Dr. John Fischer. 196 pages.

978-1880226902    **LB43**    $13.99

---

## The World To Come *A Portal to Heaven on Earth*
—Derek Leman

An insightful book, exposing fallacies and false teachings surrounding this extremely important subject... paints a hopeful picture of the future and dispels many non-biblical notions. Intriguing chapters: Magic and Desire, The Vision of the Prophets, Hints of Heaven, Horrors of Hell, The Drama of the Coming Ages. Offers a fresh, but old, perspective on the world to come, as it interacts with the prophets of Israel and the Bible. 110 pages.

978-1880226049    **LB67**    .$9.99

---

## Hebrews Through a Hebrew's Eyes
—Dr. Stuart Sacks

Written to first-century Messianic Jews, this epistle, understood through Jewish eyes, edifies and encourages all. 119 pages. Endorsed by Dr. R.C. Sproul and James M. Boice.

978-1880226612    **LB23**    $10.99

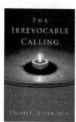

## The Irrevocable Calling *Israel's Role As A Light To The Nations*
—Daniel C. Juster, Th.D.

Referring to the chosen-ness of the Jewish people, Paul, the Apostle, wrote "For God's free gifts and his calling are irrevocable" (Rom. 11:29). This messenger to the Gentiles understood the unique calling of his people, Israel. So does Dr. Daniel Juster, President of Tikkun Ministries Int'l. In *The Irrevocable Calling*, he expands Paul's words, showing how Israel was uniquely chosen to bless the world and how these blessings can be enjoyed today. Endorsed by Dr. Jack Hayford, Mike Bickle and Don Finto. 64 pages.

978-1880226346    **LB66**    $8.99

---

## Are There Two Ways of Atonement?
—Dr. Louis Goldberg

Here Dr. Louis Goldberg, long-time professor of Jewish Studies at Moody Bible Institute, exposes the dangerous doctrine of Two-Covenant Theology. 32 pages.

978-1880226056    **LB12**    $4.99

---

## Awakening *Articles and Stories About Jews and Yeshua*
—Arranged by Anna Portnov

Articles, testimonies, and stories about Jewish people and their relationship with God, Israel, and the Messiah. Includes the effective tract, "The Most Famous Jew of All." One of our best anthologies for witnessing to Jewish people. Let this book witness for you! Russian version also available. 110 pages.

| | | | |
|---|---|---|---|
| English | 978-1880226094 | **LB15** | $6.99 |
| Russian | 978-1880226018 | **LB14** | $6.99 |

---

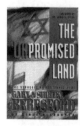

## The Unpromised Land *The Struggle of Messianic Jews Gary and Shirley Beresford*
—Linda Alexander

They felt God calling them to live in Israel, the Promised Land. Wanting nothing more than to live quietly and grow old together in the country of refuge for all Jewish people, little did they suspect what events would follow to try their faith. The fight to make *aliyah*, to claim their rightful inheritance in the Promised Land, became a battle waged not only for themselves, but also for Messianic Jews all over the world that wish to return to the Jewish homeland. Here is the true saga of the Beresford's journey to the land of their forefathers. 216 pages.

978-1880226568    **LB19**    $9.99

## Death of Messiah  *Twenty fascinating articles that address a subject of grief, hope, and ultimate triumph.*
—Edited by Kai Kjaer-Hansen

This compilation, written by well-known Jewish believers, addresses the issue of Messiah and offers proof that Yeshua—the true Messiah—not only died, but also was resurrected! 160 pages.

978-1880226582     **LB20**     $ 8.99

## Beloved Dissident *(A Novel)*
—Laurel West

A gripping story of human relationships, passionate love, faith, and spiritual testing. Set in the world of high finance, intrigue, and international terrorism, the lives of David, Jonathan, and Leah intermingle on many levels--especially their relationships with one another and with God. As the two men tangle with each other in a rising whirlwind of excitement and danger, each hopes to win the fight for Leah's love. One of these rivals will move Leah to a level of commitment and love she has never imagined--or dared to dream. Whom will she choose? 256 pages.

978-1880226766     **LB33**     $ 9.99

## Sudden Terror
—Dr. David Friedman

Exposes the hidden agenda of militant Islam. The author, a former member of the Israel Defense Forces, provides eye-opening information needed in today's dangerous world.

Dr. David Friedman recounts his experiences confronting terrorism; analyzes the biblical roots of the conflict between Israel and Islam; provides an overview of early Islam; demonstrates how the United States and Israel are bound together by a common enemy; and shows how to cope with terrorism and conquer fear. The culmination of many years of research and personal experiences. This expose will prepare you for what's to come! 160 pages.

978-1880226155     **LB49**     $ 9.99

## It is Good! *Growing Up in a Messianic Family*
—Steffi Rubin

Growing up in a Messianic Jewish family. Meet Tovah! Tovah (Hebrew for "Good") is growing up in a Messianic Jewish home, learning the meaning of God's special days. Ideal for young children, it teaches the biblical holidays and celebrates faith in Yeshua. 32 pages to read & color.

978-1880226063     **LB11**     $ 4.99